BUSINESS
TECHNOLOGY

A GUIDE
FOR MIDSIZE AND SMALL BUSINESS

MICHAEL W. JOHNSON

WAIN Technologies, LLC

Published by WAIN Technologies, LLC Jersey City, New Jersey

Editor: Karen Mafundikwa

ISBN- 13: 978-0-615-29921-1

2009930307

Printed in the United States of America

10   9   8   7   6   5   4   3   2   1

To
Maria, Nuria & Tariq

And to my parents Evon and Joy

Table of Contents

CHAPTER 6
NEW BUSINESS MEDIUM TECHNOLOGIES 141

CHAPTER 7
EMERGING AND FUTURE TECHNOLOGIES - THE WORLD CHANGES 153

ACKNOWLEDGMENTS

It is not an easy task to produce a book of decent quality. I have gained a new-found respect for writers, editors, contributors, reviewers, designers, and everyone involved in the book creation process.

I would like to thank the many friends, colleagues and clients who helped with input, feedback, critique and continued encouragement. Specifically, thanks go out to Felix Fermin, Chioma Nelson, Doug Tecle and Donna Redwood for taking the time to give the book a full read, providing me with good perspectives and additional food for thought while the manuscript was being revised. Peer review for this type of book is critical to keeping the quality high and to staying true to the book's objective. For this, I'd like to extend my thanks to Amy Siegel, an esteemed colleague whose valued feedback kept me on point. During final revisions when issues with graphics threatened to push back the release date, Denise Gehrung provided her expertise and quickly got me back on track. Much thanks to her. Additional special thanks go out to my editor, Karen Mafundikwa, for the excruciatingly painstaking detailed edits done on the book. Finally I'd like to thank Maria Anguera de Sojo who had the unenviable task of being the first to read and review the first full draft of the manuscript.

PREFACE

WHY READ THIS BOOK

Anyone over the age of 40 will be able to remember when midsize and small business technology was mostly limited to a fax machine, a phone, a photocopier, a few basic calculators and an electronic typewriter or two. Anything more sophisticated was the preserve of large companies with the associated financial resources. In the past two decades new technology has increasingly created a level playing field for midsize and small businesses competing against large companies. The drivers of this change include the arrival of readily accessible computing, and the Internet. Many customers now look to research, source and trade electronically, which means that the traditional large business with its multiple bricks-and-mortar outlets, no longer has a near monopoly of a business sector simply because it is able to saturate the market with a physical presence in cities and towns. Thanks to the Internet, the public face of a small business can, to a customer, be indistinguishable from that of a multi-billion dollar corporate empire. This equality in direct-to-customer interaction has previously never been achievable.

Over the same period of this technological revolution, business culture and customer behavior have also shifted dramatically. The characteristics one normally associates with smaller businesses, such as individuality, flexibility, uniqueness and personal service, are now highly appealing concepts to 21st century customers. These business attributes are now far more marketable than the big business equivalents of mass, volume, brand and standardization. These technological and cultural changes have converged to create opportunities for smaller businesses that never existed before. Yet, to exploit these opportunities, midsize and small businesses must understand the basic concepts of technology. They must have a decent grasp of the current and evolving technological landscape. They must, at a minimum, have some general idea of the scope of capabilities that technology offers. If they do not, then the fact that the playing field is now level for all sizes of businesses will be academic – they will be left sitting in the changing room as the game gets underway.

SCANDALS & CRISES – CUSTOMERS DEMAND CHANGE

The big is beautiful business view held strong for many decades, peaking approximately in the 1980's. Mergers, acquisitions, standardization, globalization and unfettered growth – all these were regarded as the definition of success during this era. Then came the various economic crunches of 1989 and 1992, the late 1990's market blips, and the more earth-shattering financial scandals and disasters of 2008 and 2009. The public began to see the giant companies as not only vulnerable, as evidenced by the numbers that collapsed, but also that in some cases they had been incompetently run – sometimes to the extent of operating against the interest of their customers, staff, stockholders and the public at large. The increasing public consciousness of environmental issues over the same period also generated growing customer unease about certain big business practices and their social and environmental effects. Media coverage of companies off-shoring their production or buying raw materials from organizations that were depleting rainforests fuelled an ever more pronounced cultural change in customer demand.

In the years leading up to the millennium and shortly thereafter, consumers started demanding things that they felt smaller businesses could provide - uniqueness, personalized products and services and a more direct customer experience. It became clear that midsize and small business had the ability to quickly adapt to service the ever-fluctuating market demand – something big business could not match easily. This was evidenced by the proliferation of independent record labels in the music industry, small biotechs in the pharma industry, boutiques in the retail clothing industry, and so on. And right along with the social and economic changes, technology was now making those small businesses reachable. In the past, when one wanted to buy from a small business specialist 500 miles away, you were stuck with mail order or telephone dealing. And neither method is very satisfactory or fast.

But moving into the end of the first decade of the 21st century, technology erased distance so that 500 miles is the same as 5000 miles and both are the same as right next door. Even the tiniest Mom & Pop business now has a potential *global* reach, equivalent to the largest multi-national. That little record store in Memphis can now compete with Virgin records on a national and/or global level. All a small business needs is the know-how to use technology to erase distance and operate efficiently. The customers are ready, willing and waiting!

SMALL BUSINESSES REACT TO NEW OPPORTUNITIES

This combination of technological, social and economic shifts has created a fertile field for the small business, though it must also be acknowledged that the opportunities are not always being grasped. Some have seen and embraced technology as a way of driving their business forward – delivering their products and services wrapped in the small business packaging that will make them attractive to potential customers, but providing their services on a global scale. Many of these successful smaller companies have used technology to not only lift themselves to the same plateau as their large competitors, but to actually surpass them in some cases. Smaller businesses often have the advantage of no existing massive investment in old technology to protect or wrestle with.

They have been light on their feet and have embraced technology as a way of expanding their business. Some of these small businesses have seen vast benefits as a result. Their costs have fallen or remained steady as the business grew and their customer numbers, income and profitability have risen. Some have become household names within a few months. In fact, some have become better known and more profitable than the former large companies in the same field! Such companies are now reaping the benefits of this early and well managed entry into this technological new world.

INTENDED AUDIENCE

For midsize and small business with very little technology experience or understanding, this book will be an invaluable reference guide to technology and a source of ideas on how to exploit it. It is not for the technology savvy, as it assumes the reader has limited knowledge of the available range of business technologies. While the discussions on *how* technology can be best used by the business will be useful for people of any technical ability, the descriptions *of* various business technologies are designed for people who are somewhat unfamiliar with the range of business technologies. It is not a do-it-yourself manual – rather it is intended to facilitate an understanding of business technology. After reading this book, business owners will have a broad understanding of the available technology capabilities, in order to help them formulate the use of technologies in their businesses and to have a good grounding when their technology strategy is being developed. We will mention when a business should seek outside, expert help.

This book is not intended to replace the expert advice of a seasoned business technologist who should be consulted to create a good technology strategy for the business.

In this book the author, Michael Johnson, utilizes his many years of experience in technology to explain how this technological revolution can be used as a business advantage. Jargon is explained and de-mystified, key components of the technology landscape are discussed and clarified, and sample technology configurations are provided. When equipped with this level of information, the midsize and small business owner can effectively participate in determining how technology will be used to transform and grow the business. This book is essential reading for any midsize and small business that wishes to survive and prosper in the technological 21st century world.

ABOUT THE AUTHOR

Michael Johnson has held a number of senior positions in business technology functions including Director of Technology for a large multinational company. He holds a Bachelors from New York Institute of Technology and an MBA from Columbia University Graduate School of Business. He has in-depth knowledge of financial systems, application and web development, and data & document management from over 15 years of professional experience. He has served in the role of Infrastructure Liaison and a Global Technology Solutions Partner. He also has practical experience in the operations of small businesses as the owner of a bar and lounge in Barcelona, Spain and a small record company in NYC. He currently provides technology consultancy services to businesses and non-profit organizations.

Business Technology

CHAPTER 1

INTRODUCTION

The world of business is rarely an easy place to survive and prosper – for anyone. In the past, it was often easier to see the businesses that were successful and going places than it is today - at least in theory. In previous decades one could form a crude equation along the lines of bigger = better = more successful = safer. It was not always strictly correct, but by and large, it held true, and it was held to be so by popular business culture from the mid 20th century onwards. The large business entities occupying blocks of major cities or with huge retail outlets in every out-of-town mall were the model of business success. They alone could afford the personnel and technology to provide the products and services customers demanded, while maintaining the capability to expand and continuously grow their businesses. Loved by lenders, investors and the majority of customers alike, large corporations thrived. Profits, returns, capital, debts, uniqueness and service ethics – all these traditional expectations of business became secondary considerations in the drive for size in some industries and the apparent success that size reflected.

By contrast, during the same period, the outlook for many smaller businesses was less rosy. Popular culture may have portrayed them as homely and folksy, politicians may have described them in almost heroic terms as the business backbone of the country and statistically they may even have generated a significant proportion of the nation's wealth, but in a sense, none of this mattered. The harsh reality was that many smaller businesses struggled badly during the latter decades of the 20th century. Government statistics suggest that 80% of all new small business failed within the first year. Getting access to venture capital or loans was always difficult, technology was misunderstood and frequently unaffordable, personnel numbers always had to be kept low, and there was no way that the average small businesses could possibly compete with the public relations and advertising budgets of their much larger peers. As a result they struggled to attract and retain customers and staff and their future was frequently uncertain.

Now things have changed. Today the outlook for the correctly positioned midsize and small business is very different and, more importantly, very attractive. It is necessary to look at why the position for small businesses has changed so radically in recent years in both a business and technology context.

For any business, technology should always be seen in a business context!

TECHNOLOGY BECOMES A COMMODITY

Going into the late 1980's, more advanced technology was used mainly in big businesses. Technology used in midsize and small businesses was either traditional "old-tech" such as phones, faxes and copiers or embryonic "new-tech" such as early business PCs, scanners, word processors and modems – all used mainly in office administration. One major characteristic of much of the technology of the period was its relatively high cost. Another even less admirable aspect of the arriving "new-tech" was that, to put it bluntly, it often failed to work! One box would not connect to another box as some boxes used different cable connectors or communication systems. Software systems were incompatible with each other and it could be difficult or even impossible to find someone who could fix a problem when it arose. Many mid-size, small and even some large business of this period still regarded much of the new-tech as a dark art best kept in the garage, garden shed or just about anywhere other than their business!

During the 1990's this position changed as standards were developed and implemented. Improved production and commercial arrangements meant that not only did the new technologies finally start to work together consistently but their capabilities increased exponentially. Technology began to move out of the domain of office support and into that of mainstream business function. As manufacturers became increasingly more efficient, production and retail costs for new technology plummeted in real terms. For perhaps the first time ever, the midsize and small business had the option of procuring business revolutionizing technology of a high standard that was previously available only to large companies, at basic business commodity prices. These businesses suddenly had access to technology that was equivalent to, and in some cases superior to, those that the large companies relied upon. Although this was a huge step in leveling the playing field, this availability and proliferation of technology also created its own issues for the midsize and small business.

Unfortunately, equally large numbers of small businesses have not joined in this revolution due to a mixture of fear and confusion as they survey the apparently bewildering world of technology before them. Jargon, flashy salespeople, incomprehensible publicity materials, hundreds of different ads on TV all saying that their "XYZ" box or software is the best – and of course those constant horror stories of scams, frauds, ID theft and Internet robbery. All these negatives have combined to make some small businesses regard technology as an obstacle rather than a necessity to their success. Small businesses in this category are not only missing out on a unique opportunity, but they may well be putting their very survival at risk.

SMALL BUSINESS AND 21ST CENTURY TECHNOLOGY

Let's begin by looking at what makes up a typical 21st century midsize or small business. In some ways, it is not very different from a large business. It doesn't matter much whether the business is manufacturing widgets or cakes, selling or buying, or operating as a travel agency. Every business will have certain functional business requirements. Every business big or small has to take something (raw materials, goods, skills etc) do something to it/them, and then persuade someone to buy it/them. This is how a business functions at its simplest level. Even a "Mom and Pop" business operates in this manner.

Let's look at a model of a very basic technology landscape as it may exist in any business today. That technology can, at its simplest level, be thought of in terms of functional building blocks, divided into three categories that must link to each other in order to work. The first category entails functions that relate to outward facing business activities such as marketing to customers and advertising your goods or services. These are the technology products and services that allow you, via your public face, to communicate with and market to the outside world. They are used and seen by a business and its customers / suppliers alike.

The second category of technology includes those products or services that support the core functions of a business to increase business efficiency. These functions are typically used only by the business itself and may be entirely invisible to the outside world. This includes technology components that exist to deliver day-to-day business administrative or operational support, such as payroll or tax programs, manufacturing control, accounting, printing and faxing etc.

The third category of technology can be thought of as the methods by which you conduct business transactions – transactions between you and customers and even between you and suppliers. This third category includes receiving payments, sending orders, and managing the flow of invoices and receipts.

A business needs to broadly understand technology to determine how it can be deployed to gain business advantage.

Thinking about technology in terms of these categories will be a very useful foundation as we go further. It is of course artificial and sometimes misleading to draw lines between components in these two models. In business those "business efficiency functions" may involve contact with the external world or customer visits. In technology a system that is used to electronically store documents primarily for administrative purposes may also offer customers the ability to search on-line for a given document. In reality the lines between these functional blocks are fuzzy and overlap, but more of that later. For the time being they're a good starting point for our technology discussion.

> All technology processes must be seen and understood in business equivalent terms.

This is important because sometimes technology terminology can confuse people. Try to follow along with this piece of techno-speak:

> *"Potential customers can utilize pre-set selection criteria to formulate a query to run against the repository to extract and display matching entries."*

Interesting as that sounds, and it is an example of some of the language used by some technologists, it can be expressed far more simply in business terms by saying that the customer is allowed to select available products on the company's website page.

WHAT IS BUSINESS TECHNOLOGY

Whether the technology is a laptop (hardware) or a website (software), from a business point of view it must be a component of one of the three basic building blocks functions – communication technologies, business efficiency technologies, or business medium technologies. We will expand upon this simple overview by looking at some of these components in detail in upcoming chapters to see how they may fit into the profile of a midsize and small business. Before starting this, it's worth spending a little time thinking about what is or is not necessary technology for a small business.

> The specific technology requirements of each business are unique and need to be defined by the business itself – with expert help.

There is sometimes a tendency by well-meaning technologists to encourage a "one size fits all" model for their particular areas of expertise. This usually runs along the lines of "all small businesses need to install at least XYZ." This is quite simply wrong. It should be evident that the technology requirements of a one-person watch repair business may be significantly different from that of say a small taxi company with six employees and three vehicles based in two different locations. They both may need a telephone, fax, copier and printer, and most likely a computer, an Internet connection and a few others to be discussed later. Beyond those basics everything else would be up for discussion. As an example, it seems unlikely that the watch repairer would require a local network to be setup on the premises and the taxi company would not need the kind of supplier database that a watch shop requires.

Given the advances in today's technology, expert help is a necessity, particularly when deciding on how to use new technologies that directly affect business processes. This is because the degree to which even the smallest businesses can connect their far flung offices and employees is quite simply unprecedented. Midsize and small business should make the most effective use of these new communication technologies.

> Modern technology now means there are few if any limitations on what an employee can do "out and about" as opposed to "in the office."

This is revolutionizing many areas of business operation. From sales staff spending too much time in the office because they need access to files and information, right up to field engineers, there are now many employees of companies who rarely see their office base. They never need to! Of course, this is not necessarily the correct business model for every company. Not every small business will be running a virtual office. Similarly, every small business does not need a fully integrated operations management software package that ties directly into an e-commerce database. Business technology can do wonderful, amazing things – but only if you actually need it.

> Buying technology for the sake of technology usually leads to disaster!

That particular top of the line hand-held device may appear super-sexy and impress friends, family and associates. But if it doesn't link to the business's systems, then all one has is a *very* expensive mobile phone and camera. Like every other business purchase, technology purchasing decisions should be made using a benefit analysis. We will talk about this more later when we talk about minimizing risks associated with business technology. As an entertaining side-note, we will also point out a few things to keep in mind.

- *As in many areas of life, the cheapest is rarely the best*
- *Buying the most expensive does not guarantee the best results*
- *Within one to two years there may be one that is cheaper and better*
- *The "sexiest" in appearance may not be the best*

SUMMARY

Technology for any business must be tied directly to its business needs, both from an operations perspective (run my business at its most optimal) and from a strategic perspective (position my business to lead in its category, enabling new ideas and innovation). Technology is not a separate entity – it is one more weapon in your armory to make your business the best it can be. You should always consider any new technology for your business using this view. Therefore to understand exactly what technology is required for a specific small business, one has to understand that single business including its markets and customers, and its strengths and weaknesses. You must identify the opportunities that the business has, as well as the threats it faces and align these to each technology solution. As a result, no book can provide the definitive technology template for any given business.

What this guide does is describe available technologies that are relevant or potentially relevant to midsize and small business. Some are already utilized, while others are mostly available and marketed to big business until recently. Then we'll show some representative scenarios of a small business. With each successive scenario, we will increase the business complexity and see how this introduces the potential for new technology to increase efficiency and enable growth. We will show this in a series of case studies in Chapter 10. But first, we will look at common business technologies to develop our technology vocabulary. With this basic vocabulary under our belt, we'll look at each of the three core components of our technology landscape by discussing the available technologies in each component. We need to understand these technologies before we can use them – understand how they work, how they work together, and how these technologies are important to any business.

Since we cover some topics that have been discussed for many years, please feel free to skip those with which you are comfortable.

PART I

THE LANDSCAPE OF BUSINESS TECHNOLOGY

CHAPTER 2

COMMON BUSINESS TECHNOLOGIES

T o run a business today, you need to have some basic business terminology at the very start, then build on this foundation going forward. For instance, it would be hard to get far if you didn't understand what invoice means. You may also have serious difficulties in getting anywhere if words such as customer, supplier, costs, sales, and cash flow mean little or nothing. In other words, to even start a small business you need a basic business vocabulary. Over time this vocabulary may expand to include things such as receivables, inventory management, venture capital, margins, capitalization, depreciation and other more complicated terms, if they are needed. As your business grows, so will your business vocabulary. Technology is no different – to best deploy technology in your business, you need to have a basic technology vocabulary.

This is often where a problem arises. Many people are deterred by technology terms, not surprising given the way technology is advertised. But technical terminology should be thought about in business terms. There is no need to think of them as technical terms – they are simply the proper words to describe certain technology for your business. So let's review some commonly used business

29

technologies.

THE PERSONAL COMPUTER (PC)

FIGURE 2.1 Personal computers come in many and varied shapes and sizes

It is sometimes difficult to imagine a world before computers. The advent of the personal computer (PC) and the subsequent spread of the World Wide Web have forever changed the way that companies conduct business.

To make sure that the PC functions successfully, there is a single master program that supervises all the others. This is called the operating system. In the vast majority of cases, this operating system is a Microsoft product called either Windows. Over nearly a quarter of a century, Microsoft's operating system and "The Standard PC" have achieved virtual global domination. The vast majority of PC products and systems work on these types of PCs. There is one other major PC manufacturer that does things slightly differently. These are the PCs manufactured by Apple Inc, commonly called Macs. They utilize an operating system called OS X rather than Windows. They are typically used by the more creative functions within a given business (graphic design for example).

This distinction is important. Why? Well, Microsoft due to its global dominance has been the defacto computer operating system for business operations whereas Apple with its Mac is the King/Queen of the creative world. This sharp line has started to blur in recent years, and almost all software designed to run on a windows PC can now operate on an Apple as well. With this in mind, the content of this book is highly relevant for both businesses that operate with Apple computers as well as Windows-based PCs.

While it isn't necessary to detail how a computer operates, there are some things worth understanding when you take ownership of this technology.

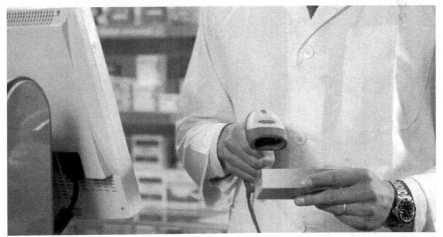

FIGURE 2.2 The personal computer is now an indispensible tool for business

At the end of the day selecting a PC (Windows or Apple) usually involves looking at your business requirements. It is highly unlikely that a top-of-the-line PC would be required for a typical small business, though this may not end up being a major factor as the cost differentials between "low end" and "high end" PCs are ever smaller. It is advisable to look for large amounts of disk space and memory. Also, PCs that use the latest and most powerful chip technology will offer a longer-term investment than others. Keep in mind that many PCs become obsolete within 2-4 years of purchase. It doesn't mean they will stop working – but they will struggle to cope with the versions of software that will be around in four or five years' time. It's worth checking with an expert for specific advice prior to purchase and planning for upgrading at certain periods of your business's growth.

MOBILE COMPUTING

FIGURE 2.3 Smartphones & laptops are two mobile computing technologies

Today's business world is mobile due to a number of factors. The high cost of city center premises means business people now wish to reduce these overheads in square feet terms by not necessarily providing a desk for every employee every day – particularly for people in say sales who spend a lot of time 'on the road'. Major social changes also mean that people wish to work from home more since technology now permits them to do so. Views on productivity have changed and more is required of employees as time goes on. The days when someone out of the office on a training course or client site visit was unreachable and unable to deal with an issue until they returned, are now long gone. Many customers also expect more from a supplier's visit than a general chat followed up by a lunch and the promise of "*I'll check that out when I get back to my office*". Customers now increasingly demand that their suppliers arrive on site with the capability to work alongside them and make things happen then and there.

All of these factors have led to increasing business demand for the office base to be portable and capable of following staff around as they move from one location to another. Technology has evolved to meet the need and now provides the ability for someone who needs to travel to pretty much take their office with them. The cell phone is well known and familiar to virtually all, but what is perhaps less broadly understood is how powerful and flexible mobile computing has become. There are really three key components to think about in this area if you plan to take your office with you when out and about.

1. What sort of mobile device capability you'll need
2. How you'll connects to the wider world
3. What systems and facilities back at home base you will need to be able to access.

There are a vast number of devices to choose from. In general, what you need will depend upon your business needs and personal preferences and you may find that professional advice will be highly useful. As an example, if your need is to access only emails, diary and the Internet when out of the office, then devices such as smart phones and personal organizers may be right for you.

On the other hand, if you plan to access and update your office's inventory and accounting systems etc, then you'll probably need a slim line, lightweight PC (sometimes called a laptop or netbook) with a larger, more conventional screen and keyboard to make it easier to work alongside your client. The really good news is that connecting a portable device to the wider world such as the Internet is now very easy. Most of these devices come with built-in wireless connectivity so that you only have to switch it on to be connected. Having said that, there are still rural areas without the microwave network coverage that permits wireless connectivity and in these cases you may still need to find a telephone or network socket to plug your mobile PC into. Once again, specialist advice will tell you what you need based on your locations and patterns of usage.

Finally, some of your systems at your base may need to be made available so that they can be accessed from a remote location. This is rarely complicated for many facilities such as email, but in other cases, such as accounting systems, inventory, document imaging etc, some specialist help may be required. The recent advances in mobile and communication technologies mean that, these days, the effort needed to produce a mobile extension to the office is insignificant. The financial and time investment required is usually modest and the benefits can be significant.

Let's consider the example of a small engineering company that makes components for the automotive industry. Until a decade or so ago their products were sold on a traditional basis. A sales rep/engineer would usually visit a client to be briefed on their needs. He would take the details and return to the office. The details were fed into the company's master systems, which produced a technical drawing. The representative then went back to the client with the drawing for discussion and approval. He then returned to his office to make any changes and the details were input into their systems to produce a new drawing and a quotation. Yes, you've guessed it, at that stage the quotation and revised drawing were taken back to the client's office for final signoff and order generation or, more commonly, more changes.

This process could take several weeks and involve 3-6 client site visits on average and dozens of faxes. It was not that the systems were slow. The main delays were caused by trying to arrange the multiple visits and calendar co-ordination between the company and its clients. Today, this process is almost always concluded in one visit and at a maximum of around one hour's duration. The client and representative input all the details directly into the supplier's base systems through a mobile PC. As a result, the drawings are generated and can be viewed on-line or directly printed at the client's site. Any changes required by the client can be immediately entered and a revised drawing produced. When the client is satisfied, the mobile PC then accesses the quotations system to generate the price. The final contract can also be generated and signed on the spot if the client is willing.

The time and cost saved here over the old approach is phenomenal. Both new business acquisition and client retention have significantly improved for those businesses employing these technologies. Similar benefits are usually achievable in most businesses if the technology is correctly applied. For many small businesses this technology is well worth thinking about. It could revolutionize the way they do business.

LAPTOPS, NOTEBOOKS & NETBOOKS

Many laptops now carry processing power and disk space that is indistinguishable from that of desktop computers. The basic components of a laptop (CPU, memory, hard drive) are the same as that of a desktop. Additionally the recent improvements in screen technology mean that some of the readability issues that were traditionally associated with some laptops have long been resolved – the quality of the screens nowadays is superb. In fact, the only difference between the LCD screen on your laptop and the LCD screen used for a PC is that the PC screen is bigger.

FIGURE 2.4 Notebooks have grown significantly in recent years

Some businesses use their laptops as the office machine and simply take them with them when out and about. Using wireless technology, these types of computers can now offer mobile Internet connection to services. In general the smaller the laptop, the more expensive it is, assuming all other aspects of the specification are identical with the average weight of a modern laptop range from three to eleven pounds.

FIGURE 2.5 Laptops have extended beyond the confines of the office

The terms notebook and laptop tend to be used interchangeably. Netbooks on the other hand, are extremely low-cost notebooks with extremely basic capabilities (word processing, email, and web browsing) and are more akin to handhelds. Laptops have LCD screens that range from 11 to 17 inches, whereas netbooks have screens of 10 inches and under. The portability of a laptop or netbook is based on its rechargeable battery. Today's laptops rely on lithium-ion (Li-ion) batteries, with lifespan of up to five years and can last up to eight hours. Lower end laptops come with nickel metal hydride (NiMH) batteries which provide a much shorter life for the laptop and must be factored in when considering acquisition.

While its portability remains a key feature, its size makes it ideal for use in smaller businesses. Because they are self-contained units, laptops are great for saving space and being unaffected by power outages. Laptop computers are generally more expensive than desktop systems, even though they provide the same level of performance. Consider as well that it can be difficult to customize or upgrade a laptop, because it is an all-in-one device.

With the wide range of models available, a laptop can cost anywhere from $400 to $3000 and up. The top manufacturers for laptops are Hewlett-Packard (HP), Dell, Gateway, Lenovo and Acer. However there are hundreds of excellent laptops on the market. Many laptops typically come with 14 to 17 inch screens, and notebooks will 11 to 13 inch screens. The Dell XPS is a well-known laptop and HP's Pavilion is also well worth a look. Acer and Sony also produce excellent models and have a reputation for reliability. For smaller notebooks, The Lenovo IdeaPad is getting good press. The Sony VAIO range is also well regarded as a trendsetter in this area. Tablet PCs, with their touch screen interface, have become mainstays for business people who have to work in the field. Some of the most rugged are the Panasonic Toughbook line, although these are quite pricey. A cheaper but still reliable option is the HP Pavilion or the Lenovo ThinkPad. Netbooks only really made a splash on the market in late 2007, but have become one of the fastest growing computer markets. The most popular brands in this category are the Asus PC, the Acer Aspire One and the Dell Inspiron Mini.

SMARTPHONES

Interestingly enough this term is one that is used widely within the technology world yet has no true definition. For some it is a mobile phone with PC like capabilities. For others it represents a complex platform capable of evolving over time. Ultra-portable devices started with Personal Data Assistants (PDAs), which arrived in the 1980's and were usually akin to a pocket electronic diary. They were primarily intended for keeping lists of phone numbers or calendar appointments.

Then, early in the millennium, the hand-held computer was released. Also referred to as netbooks or tablet PCs, these devices as discussed before, have many (but not all) of the capabilities of laptop PCs. It didn't take the technology industry long to realize that it made little sense for people to carry 3 or 4 separate hand-held devices, with overlapping capabilities that were often broadly similar to each other. During this decade, these devices have not only become vastly more powerful and sophisticated, they have also converged in functional terms.

FIGURE 2.6 Smartphones are essential tools for sales people

On the whole, smartphones are increasingly very powerful hand-held PCs, regardless of brand. There are many on the market now. For many businesses, an ideal device is one that is capable of accessing the Internet through wireless connections, access office administrative systems for uploading and downloading files, and can make telephone calls. Functionality such as cameras and the ability to run office applications on the smartphone may be desirable rather than essential. Some of these devices have excellent screens in terms of visibility and clarity but remember there is a relationship to effectiveness and size. The tiniest models may look cute, but are their tiny screens really practical?

There's not much point having access to the Internet if the pages displayed are on such a small screen that they can barely be read. The choice of model and user interface – touch screen stylus-input or mini-keyboard – will remain a matter of personal preference. But again, the same caveats with respect to usability apply. So for the immediate future it may be advisable to consider that a laptop computer may still be required for _serious_ off-site work. Don't expect your employees to enjoy typing up expense reports on their smartphones!

When selecting a smartphone there are certain key things to look for. Obviously size and weight are an issue, but you also need to decide if you want a touch-screen or a full miniature keyboard. And these days, having full access to the Internet on your smartphone is essential. Particularly important is the operating system the phone is capable of running and what facilities it provides. Being able to run a version of Windows for smartphones can be highly advantageous – that way your smartphone will run all the same applications you use on your laptop or desktop PC.

Other available operating systems are Palm OS, Symbian OS and BlackBerry. At the time of writing the Apple iPhone has been making all the news. This is an incredibly powerful and flexible device offering a range of facilities not dreamt of only a few years ago. It is driven by a touch screen interface. From an iPhone it is possible to surf the web, use GPS (global positioning system) to find a location and routes, run applications such as calendar management, take photos, download and play music and make phone calls! It should offer around five hours of talk time from its battery.

There are some other excellent smartphones that are just as popular in the market. Samsung's OMNIA phone offers similar functionality. The Palm Treo Pro and AT&T Tilt offer the same powerful functions but come with a built in small QWERTY keyboard – invaluable to people that need to send lots of text. The Blackberry range is making a huge impact due to its powerful functionality, excellent design and built in keyboards. It made the news in early 2009 when President Obama refused to give up his Blackberry when he took office. That is how essential they have become to some people! All of these devices have slightly varying capabilities and prices vary considerably based on the phone and the service plan.

SUPPORT FOR HARDCOPIES

Much as the world would like to move away from paperwork, it still plays an important part in basic business transactions. For at least half a century people have been trying to achieve the paperless office.

Sadly, only modest progress has been made. Once a business needs to put something on paper, such as an invoice, you have to be able to deal with that piece of paper in an electronic way. Either it is a digital file that needs to be printed, or it is an original copy that needs to be scanned and saved to a document management collection. No matter what, every business needs most, if not all of the following technologies to deal with the ever present "paper" office.

PRINTERS

Modern printers are capable of printing reports, letters, graphics or high-quality photographs in monochrome or color. There are two types of printers, inkjet and laser. Inkjet printers use dye cartridges of three or five different colors. They can print great pictures, although they tend to not print text so well.

On the other hand, laser printers use toner that is melted onto the paper during printing. This means text is really sharp and crisp – but most affordable laser printers only print in black and white. Color laser printers are available and are getting cheaper, but they still don't print pictures as nicely as inkjet printers. The type of printer you get will depend on your business. Need to print a lot of text documents? Then a laser printer will be preferable. Need to make lots of beautiful graphs and images? Then you will want an inkjet printer. Need both? Well, printers are cheap enough so that many businesses end up having a printer of each type.

SCANNERS

Many companies are still in a transition phase in the way they do business – some business is conducted electronically and some is still done through paper invoices and receipts. So they tend to have important information both on the computer and on paper – not easy to keep track of! In this situation there are two choices; you can either print out all your electronic documents to store them in traditional file cabinets, or you can create electronic copies of all your paper documents and store them electronically. Either way ensures that all your important documents are in one place. These days it only makes sense to go with the second option. After all, doing business electronically is becoming more common, not less. You need a device called a scanner to convert paper documents to an electronic format. This makes a scanner an essential piece of technology for document and records management.

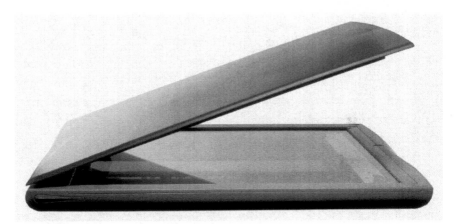

FIGURE 2.7 Scanners today, are extremely stable and very portable

A scanner works by digitizing (making a digital copy) a piece of paper. Essentially, the scanner takes an image of the piece of paper; in fact a scanner creates electronic files that are the same as a digital camera. These images can then be stored on a PC, making it much easier for the small business to keep track of its invoices, receipts and payments. Many scanners look like the top part of a photocopier – where you lift up a lid and place the document on a glass plate so that it can be scanned. Other scanners feed documents in similar to a fax machine. Both types of scanners work well, although the second type works better when you want to scan many pages of paper.

But what if you want to change some of the wording on an invoice that you received? It is difficult to change an image in that manner, but there is another tool that scanners provide – optical character recognition (OCR). With OCR, you can scan and store incoming paperwork and convert it to a text file that can be opened by programs such as Microsoft Word instead of as an image. This technology can be a lifesaver for a business that needs to electronically store supplier invoices, letters and legal documents. It also means there is an electronic copy of the paper that can be edited, archived or sent via email.

ALL-IN-ONE DEVICES

Midsize and small business often means tight budgets, making large photocopiers and separate printers and scanners expensive. One way to reduce overall costs is to consolidate printing, faxing, and copying utilities into a multifunctional device – usually called an all-in-one. Although some all-in-ones have more limited capabilities than their standalone counterparts, most of today's all-in-one devices offer high performance at excellent without the unnecessary bells and whistles of a high end printer or scanner.

An all-in-one always has a printer and a scanner together, effectively turning it into a copier. Many all-in-ones also have faxing and at higher price points, features such as automatic duplexing (printing both sides), network connectivity, and extra paper trays. Multi-function printers are available in the low-, mid-, and high-end range. Low-end devices are usually small enough to rest on a desk top and can be used with letter size documents that fit within the document feeder. Low-end all-in-ones are usually inkjet based and may or may not have fax capability. Prices start at around $150.

For businesses requiring greater capabilities, mid-range multifunctional machines (costing between $2,500 and $7,000) are built around a copier machine structure – free-standing units that have extra paper trays can be connected to an office network. At the top end, a high-end multifunctional machine provides rapid print functions and advanced copying options such as sorting and stapling. However, a low or mid-range machine should be enough for almost any small business. As is the case when purchasing an individual printer or scanner, business owners should determine the volume of work that the machine will need to handle, as well as the tasks that the machine is expected to perform. It is important to remember the downside to a combined device. If one piece of the machine fails to operate, then all the other functions may not work properly. For instance, if the scanner is not working properly, then the machine will not be able to make copies. It is important to keep in mind that multifunctional machines can be expensive to repair, especially the mid and high-end models.

SHREDDERS

Shredders are becoming increasingly necessary for business owners as identity theft and business espionage becomes more common. Sales of paper shredders have increased significantly in recent years due to the passage of government information privacy acts like FACTA, HIPAA and the Gramm-Leach-Bliley Act. There are several different types of paper shredders, based on how completely they shred your documents. The most commonly found shredders on the market are cross-cut and strip-cut shredders that reduce your papers to narrow strips (strip-cut) or small square pieces (cross-cut). Strip-cut shredders are the most economical choice, with many major manufacturers –including Fellowes, Dynex and Init – offering models that start at just $50.

FIGURE 2.8 Shredders are extremely underutilized in smaller businesses

These shredders are widely available in retail outlets, but are also the least secure method of shredding. Cross-cut shredders are a bit more expensive, but still commonly available in retail outlets. There are even more secure paper shredder types on the market. These include particle-cut shredders, which create small circular or square-shaped chards, and shredders that pierce each document into small pieces before tearing the paper apart.

Other kinds of paper shredders use a mesh screen to destroy documents. Choose your shredder based on your required level of security, workflow volume, and types of material that need to be shredded. While all shredders can handle paper documents, only certain models can shred paper clips, staples, credit cards, CDs, or computer disks. Do not underestimate the value of this misunderstood and highly underutilized technology.

VIDEO PROJECTION

Every business that needs to, big or small, wants to be able to display a PowerPoint presentation, an image, or a spreadsheet during a meeting. For this you need a video projector, an almost essential tool for effective business presentations. The features you need to consider are resolution and brightness. In most cases, the display resolution is the determining price factor – the higher the resolution, the higher the price. Although it may seem like an arbitrary distinction, the human eye can generally distinguish differences in quality, especially for detailed images. Therefore a higher resolution projector definitely produces a more pleasing image to the eye.

The other price factor is based on how bright the projector can project the image, measured in lumens. General guidelines specify that small rooms in low-light settings require projectors with 1500 to 2500 lumens, medium-sized rooms with dimmed lighting need 2500 to 4000 lumens, and larger rooms with little or no lighting control need over 4000 lumens. Pick a projector based on the room you plan to use.

In contrast to traditional conference room projectors, ultra-lights are portable, lightweight projectors that are intended for mobile use. Handheld projectors are already on the market, and the price is dropping steadily – this may be a very handy marketing tool for your sales team. One other thing to keep in mind is the maintenance costs. The typical lifespan for most projector lamps is between 1,000 and 4,000 hours. Bulbs can be expensive to replace, ranging from $250 to $600. Small business owners should look for high-efficiency, high-performance lamps that use lower wattage, thereby reducing energy costs.

The highest quality video projectors are not always necessary for small office settings, especially in firms with few employees. That being said, everyone expects that even the smallest of business can provide professional looking presentations.

FIGURE 2.9 Projectors today are lightweight and mobile

TELEPHONE SYSTEMS

An effective telephone system is essential for any business, small or large. Phones have been around for a hundred years and most phone technologies have been around for decades. In any small office with more than a few people, you need a system for desk to desk calls and for transferring calls between offices.

THE OLD SYSTEMS

The traditional office telephone systems are key systems, keyless systems and PBX systems. Key systems work by connecting individual handsets with a central unit (called a key system unit or KSU), so that users can make calls to another in-office extension. Key systems are suited for companies with up to 50 employees. Keyless systems connect directly to in-office phone lines so they do not need a KSU. They work well for small businesses with fewer than 15 employees. Private branch exchange (PBX) systems are similar to key systems, but they generally offer more advanced features such as direct inward dialing and automated directory service. PBX systems have become more accessible to smaller businesses but remain most suited for companies with more than 50 employees.

THE NEW SYSTEM – VoIP

Voice over Internet Protocol (VoIP) technology is a catchall term for services that rely on a computer network (or the Internet) rather than the public switched telephone network (PTSN) to make calls. However, VoIP systems connect to the PTSN when you call normal telephone numbers. VoIP systems have gained popularity with both small and large companies over the past decade. You don't even need to throw out your old phones to use VoIP – traditional handsets can achieve VoIP service using an analog telephone adapter, which then connects to a network via an existing telephone jack.

Alternatively, organizations can purchase VoIP phones that connect directly to the network but require a separate VoIP service provider. VoIP systems feature high bandwidth and can be integrated with other web services, such as video and chat. And since VoIP is over the internet, calling other VoIP phones, anywhere in the world, is like making a local call! There is also software that can be installed on a computer in order to make VoIP calls without a separate VoIP phone. VoIP phones can also be used to talk for free over the Internet using software such as Skype and Windows Live Messenger. Because they transmit both voice and data over the same line, VoIP systems can also reduce operations costs. However, VoIP services are somewhat new and service can be unreliable without a well built network in your office.

THE NEW PBX (ROUTERS, SWITCHES AND VoIP)

PBX has become a generic term that covers the range of

telephone connection options a business may need:

- *Extension to extension dialing in the building*
- *Internal telephone conferencing (multi party)*
- *Connection to the external conventional phone system*
- *Connection of one LAN to another*
- *Connection of a LAN to a wide area network (WAN)*
- *Connection of a LAN to an ISP for Internet Access*
- *Phone calls over the Internet.*

They typically sit at the very heart of a company's communications technology. Choosing the right PBX for a given set of needs, whether key or keyless system, old PBX, or new VoIP, is something usually done with expert advice. It should be included as part of the core infrastructure design when a company is buying or upgrading its technology.

PERIPHERALS

There is a host of different pieces of electronic equipment that you can connect to a computer these days. In fact, it has become standard that every piece of electronics can "talk" to a PC! Any electronics that is designed to work while connected to a PC is called a peripheral. Printers and all-in-ones are considered peripherals and so are scanners. The standard type of connector that most peripherals use these days is the USB connector. It is also the same type of connector that most printers use and that USB flash drives use. Given the way technology is going today, the USB connector will be around for a number of years yet. So make sure that your peripheral uses this kind of connector as it will be the most versatile and the easiest to transfer between PCs. There are many, many different types of peripherals and we will review some of those more useful to a business here.

WEB CAMERAS

Increasingly, businesses are using video conferencing and any businesses unable to provide required visual eye-to-eye contact with potential or existing customers could be in danger of being perceived as having something to hide! Nowadays, you can buy video camera peripherals for a PC that are designed to send that video signal through the internet to another computer. These video cameras are known as web cameras, or more commonly, webcams. A webcam is now becoming an essential part of a minimum technology configuration. Some PCs screens, notably laptops, now have cameras, microphones and speakers built in. If yours does not, then investing a small sum of money in a camera (and a decent quality microphone for voice transmissions) will prove worthwhile.

A camera can be either a basic model dedicated to broadcasting a facial image from the desk or they can be purchased as conventional cameras that are tripod mounted so that they can provide an image of an entire room. Some cameras are even designed so that they can be rotated and moved by the person at the other end watching the video stream, while others rotate and follow a person's face automatically.

DIGITAL CAMERAS

One of the fastest changes within business technology in recent years has been the advent of and demand for images. Gone are the days when it was enough to give a verbal description over the phone and then and say "do you want it?" It is now common for customers and other businesses to demand an image of an object or to see it live during the discussion. Every digital camera can create an image in a digital format that can be downloaded from the camera onto your computer. The details behind the camera – such as what kind of sensor it has, or how many megapixels it is – does not matter for this book.

Choose a camera that has the capabilities and image resolution that suits your company's needs. What matters here is that *every* digital camera can connect to almost any computer with the right cable, and almost all cameras will connect using the USB port on the PC. As a side-note, many cameras also come with software for PCs that will let you easily manipulate and store your images. However there is also software you can purchase, such as Adobe Photoshop that can manipulate images as well.

MICROPHONES, SPEAKERS & HEADSETS

We've already mentioned microphones and speakers in relation to webcams. For businesses, this is the most common usage for these peripherals. However, if you are setting up a low-cost video conferencing system for a room, you will want to look at microphones and speakers designed for this kind of function. The microphones should have echo canceling (so you won't hear yourself speak) and, ideally, noise canceling to get rid of unwanted background sounds.

FIGURE 2.10 Headsets are very useful in customer service functions

The speakers should be suited for voice communications. This means you will not need a speaker set with a large sub woofer, for example. For one-on-one video conferencing, the best peripheral to get is a headset with an integrated microphone. Not only does this give you the privacy of a telephone – only you can hear the person speaking on the video – but the headset microphones are specifically designed to work well with voices and webcam systems. All desktop PCs and laptops have ports specifically for headsets and microphones, and this is one of the few peripherals that do not need to use the USB connector.

Web cameras, microphones, headsets and speakers are all now generally reliable devices with quite low cost. Some are of slightly higher quality than others and built to slightly higher specification. The details are best obtained from local dealers when you need to make the purchase because the models and technology available literally changes with the seasons. It's worth noting that in the past some webcams and headset microphones were known to have compatibility problems with some models of sound cards (i.e. the device inside the PC that controls the computer's sound).

This kind of problem is rare today but it is worth keeping in mind. Ask the vendor to confirm that the microphone or webcam will work with the model of PC or laptop you use.

UPS – UNINTERRUPTABLE POWER SUPPLY

When there is a power failure, not only does the coffee machine go off - the whole business can stop dead. This may be catastrophic if communications and information systems are all unavailable. Customers are not always patient and if they are unable to get service due to "sorry our systems are down", they will go elsewhere. Even in the event of having customers with unlimited patience, there is another potential problem. Modern technology is not always very happy at being shut-off in mid-flow without prior warning. It likes being closed down in an orderly manner.

Although it should not be a problem, in reality when the power comes back on, not everything may be as it was. Databases may have been left unstable, servers may refuse to re-start and communication connections refuse to communicate. One easy and relatively low-cost way of preventing these problems is to install an Uninterruptable Power Supply or UPS system. These kick in instantly in the event of a power failure and provide power to the computers for a period of time. At the very least, this can allow time to close down the computers in an orderly fashion.

This type of power backup is an excellent idea for every computer in your office. Who knows how much data may be lost on individual PC's if people were not saving their work regularly when the power went out? UPS systems are absolutely essential for your back-end computer systems and network technology. UPS systems vary greatly in price and function depending upon the business's perceptions of risks and need to operate continuously in the event of a power cut. With UPS systems more than any other piece of technology, there is no point in buying it if it will not be absolutely reliable.

APC offers a wide range of small and affordable 120/220V power supply backups systems that will suit most needs. They are a well respected name and offer an insurance policy that will pay for any equipment damaged by a power surge that was protected by one of their UPS systems.

LOCAL AREA NETWORKS

Any business using more than one PC will find it advisable to link them together in a local area network (LAN). A typical configuration may look like the above picture. Any number of PCs may be connected together to form a LAN – and this may involve designating one of them to be the server. The PCs may be joined together by several technologies including conventional cables or wireless systems. The server PC (usually referred to as a server) is the one where the master files of information are stored so that they can be shared by other PCs.

This sharing of information is one of the core concepts of modern technology. A single, standard, master source of information which is shared and utilized by many people is fundamental in any business system. As an example, it would be highly embarrassing for a staff member on the upper floor of a business to quote potential buyers one price for goods while colleagues on the lower floor are quoting another price! Therefore, the ability to see one central information file, a database, is essential. This general principle of sharing can also be applied to connections. In the past there were several types of LAN and some variations still exist, but for the most part the small business is likely to encounter two main types.

The first is the Ethernet cabled LAN. This type of conventional LAN uses cables to connect devices together. The advantage of using that system is very high transfers speeds can be achieved. Typically, a person using a database on a server that resides on another floor in the building can see little difference when compared to using a database residing on their own PC. The transfer rate and usage speed are often referred to as LAN Performance. This type of LAN is necessary when large files need to be transferred regularly between different PCs and the server. The disadvantage of cabled LANs is that they are cabled! This involves running cables around buildings and adding to the jungle of cables that sits under floors, in ducting or sometimes just scattered around the floor.

FIGURE 2.11 A typical office network is a mixture of wired and wireless

The second type of LAN is the newer wireless LAN. As the name suggests, the devices on a wireless LAN link to each other through a wireless connection and no cables are involved. This offers huge potential benefits to a business but also has a few drawbacks. On the plus side wireless LANs eliminate the need for expensive cabling activities and devices attached to them can be moved from place to place easily. On the down side, wireless LANs run at a slightly lower speed than their cabled counterparts (though this is not usually an issue for most small businesses). There are also some security issues due to the fact that wireless transmissions can be intercepted, although this is unlikely to be a serious concern in most cases. Wireless systems are, by their nature, also vulnerable to interference and "drops", i.e., a temporary loss of connection to the LAN. The basic principles of LANs and servers are very simple and they are easy to install, but designing and configuring them optimally for a given business's needs is something best done with expert advice if problems are to be avoided.

ISP & INTERNET SERVICE ENVIRONMENTS

To connect to the Internet, a PC needs some form of built-in communications and connection capability. Almost all modern PCs come with support built in for several options allowing connection to the internet. All of these methods have advantages and disadvantages. They may also have cost variations. The key point to understand at this stage is that the business does not need to worry about many of the technicalities of this. To connect to the Internet, one will usually buy the services of an Internet Service Provider or ISP. The ISP is a company that provides its customers with a connection facility to the Internet. Many will offer a range of services covering one or more Internet connection methods and also additional services such as:

- *On-line storage so that a customer can keep additional information or backups of their PC on the ISP's hard disk*
- *Email services that actually route emails from the Internet to a customer's account and allow them to download to their PCs if they wish.*
- *Security services such as virus and intrusion protection*

There are a very large number of ISPs offering a vast range of services and it is impossible to describe them all here. What can be thought about a little are the general characteristics of the above methods of connection to the ISP and therefore the wider Internet world.

FIGURE 2.12 Most cable/telephone companies provide fast, reliable ISP services

Most connections to the early Internet were via dialup modems. This method of using a telephone call to connect to an ISP is still available and the technology has the advantage of being low cost and fairly reliable. There are two downsides to using this method. First, the speed of response from the Internet to the PC is very slow by today's standards – 10 to 100 times slower than any of the other connection methods. Secondly, this method of connection is inconvenient for mobile computing with laptops because to connect to the Internet the user will need to find access to a telephone jack. A variation of this is the Digital Subscriber Line (DSL) or Asymmetric Digital Subscriber Line (ADSL) which is usually provided by the telephone company and delivers far superior connectivity and performance than that of the dialup method.

The system called wireless is a technology that has arrived in the past few years and is applied across a range of areas. As the name suggests, its primary objective is to eliminate the cable connections and wires that can be almost as much of an irritation to a small business as paperwork! In the context of ISP connections, it is now possible to have a wireless connection in the PC that allows it to find and connect to a local wireless connection point in a similar fashion to the way cell phones connect to cell towers. This means no wires are needed, the transmission speeds are relatively fast and people can take their PC with them. In some very rural or remote areas such coverage may be limited or unreliable.

A PC can also connect to the ISP and Internet via satellite. This method is for those who need mobile computing and are visiting areas without conventional wireless service coverage. One can become truly global in terms of Internet access. The downsides here are (1) additional equipment such as mini-dishes is often required to find and broadcast to the satellite and (2) connection and service costs can be high.

Finally, there is direct cable. Some urban or suburban areas that are cabled for TV or high speed telephone data also offer ISP/Internet connection via their service. While the service is very reliable, has fast speeds and often moderately priced, cable tends to be restricted to major urban areas or new suburban developments.

Competition between ISPs is fierce and there are some good deals to be had, but it makes sense to check several aspects of the deals:

1. What bandwidth are they offering? In other words, how fast will the Internet connection be for day-to-day use?
2. How much free disk space comes with the offer? Will this be sufficient for the company's needs?
3. How many mailboxes (basically email addresses) can one have?
4. What video and VoIP services do they offer?
5. How much data transfer per payment period is included free of charge?
6. Do they offer additional services such as auto-backup and restore and conventional phone services?

> 7.   How much will it cost to "upgrade" any of the above should the company's usage increase due to business growth?

SECURITY SOFTWARE

However small the business, the moment it connects to the Internet it's necessary to start thinking about the locks and bolts of security. When a PC or LAN is connected to the Internet, it becomes vulnerable to the outside world. The vulnerability arises for a number of reasons, but essentially it can be broken down into two categories.

First, when downloading from the Internet it is necessary to ensure that what is being downloaded and loaded onto the PC does not have some other program piggybacking on the download to make itself a new home on the PC's hard disk. These can be malicious programs called Trojans that can take over your computer, or viruses in emails that will run when you open the email and destroy data on your computer.

The second type of risk is having someone actually break into your network. This can happen via downloads as per the viruses above, but it can also happen when connected to certain Internet web sites. In rare circumstances, it may be possible for someone in another location anywhere in the world to take control of another PC. Security software acts in the same way as the locks and bolts on door and windows and also as a security guard on reception that stops unauthorized people from entering the building. The costs are usually small but the risk reduction huge – it is an essential investment for any PC connected to the Internet.

These risks can be virtually eliminated using security software that checks all files and emails downloaded for viruses and blocks any that are infected. Security software also contains firewalls; intrusion detection and access controls that work together to stop people in other locations from hijacking the PC. The security software also periodically sweeps the PCs hard disk and other areas looking for any uninvited software guests and eliminates them if they are found. Windows PCs and laptops also offer an update feature that allows the computer to update its own software to protect against known types of attacks. This update function should be turned on. Remember also that not all security risks are high-tech. Leaving a PC connected and unattended in a public area is a good way for a casual passerby to help himself to key information. Laptops are even more vulnerable and should always be protected by at least a password or other security system.

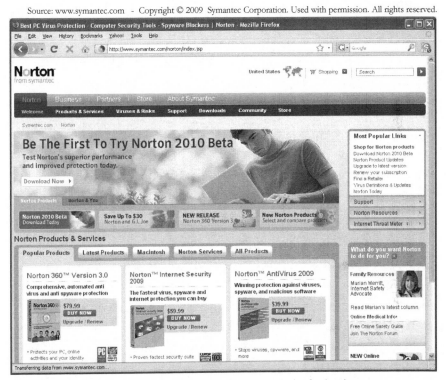

FIGURE 2.13 PC security must be of the highest priority for businesses

Most security software packages today come with anti-virus, Internet firewalls and PC optimization software included. Many also offer the ability to stop accidental intrusion by young people into Internet sites that may be unsuitable. The best-known name in this area is probably Symantec's Norton product range, which has been around for many years in one form or another. McAfee is another well known security package offering comprehensive protection for your PC.

PC MAINTENANCE

"My PC's running slow!" is a commonly heard cry of frustration in many businesses. This isn't just a nuisance – it can seriously impact your business in a number of ways. Servicing a client's phone call can be problematic if the person concerned has to wait for minutes until the PC finds the client's records. No client wants to be kept hanging on the phone because *"our system is slow today"*. Staff productivity and job satisfaction can also decline. Additionally, costs can rise. If a regular activity/task that normally should take seconds is in fact taking minutes, the cost of this multiplied through a month can be significant. Problems of this type can also lead to unnecessary capital expenditure. Buying a new, more powerful PC because an existing system is grinding along can be expensive and possibly not needed.

There could be many reasons for a PC or computer system functioning sub-optimally. It could be that you're asking more of your PC than it's capable of, especially if it has been around for a while and you're running multiple advanced programs and applications on it at the same time. Sadly, it's also true that some software companies continue to churn out software that is inefficiently written and resource hungry, meaning that their programs will, by definition, run slowly. These causes are the exception, for the most part. As a general rule, a slow running or 'freezing' PC is usually telling you that it's time to start doing some maintenance and spring-cleaning. This should not be left until you're seeing symptoms of a problem. If PC maintenance activities are carried out routinely and regularly you may help prevent the occurrence of problems.

As we discussed earlier, a modern PC system comprises dozens of pieces of software, many of which are periodically updated and replaced by newer versions. If one of your software components is out-of-date, it may not be working at optimum efficiency with other software components. It may be worth getting some expert advice on-line or in person to see whether there is anything here that's causing you grief.

The most common cause for PCs performing sub-optimally is the following. When your PC files information onto its hard disk, depending upon various circumstances, it may need to write parts of that information in different places on the disk. When you subsequently need to re-access that information, the more the computer has to search in different locations to retrieve data then the slower the retrieval and related operations will be. The more you use your computer, and the more you install new programs/software the greater the likelihood that data for a given file is spread all over the disk. This is called fragmentation and it is the root cause of most PC's sluggishness. Most operating systems and security software systems however come with what's called a de-fragmentation utility program that will help cleanup and re-organize your disk. You should run this periodically as well as configure these programs (called utilities) to run automatically on a predetermined schedule.

FIGURE 2.14 Some PC maintenance software offer extensive capabilities

The fact that many people keep vast amounts of unnecessary and obsolete information on their hard disks contributes significantly to the issue. Images and video files are particularly large. The more space that's full the more that disk fragmentation will occur and the slower your system will become. Make a point of periodically clearing out and deleting unwanted files and data etc. If necessary you can archive it to CD and store 'just in case' or utilize the backup capability that we will discuss later in this book. At minimum those un-needed or obsolete files should no longer be occupying space on your main disk. There are software programs that can help with this task.

When a program is actually doing something for you, it will be using an allocation of the memory in your computer. If you do not have sufficient memory, your operating system will try to move parts of programs that are not being used onto the hard disk until they're needed at which time it will load them back into memory. This to-ing and fro-ing is very slow and inefficient. The more of it that your PC is doing, the slower your PC will run. The solutions to this are simple. Firstly, make sure that your PC has sufficient memory to support your usage requirements. A professional can help there. If there's any doubt you can usually purchase additional memory and install it.

At the outset we said that capital expenditure might be avoidable, but unfortunately not always! Technology changes fast and much modern software needs far more memory and computer power than they did even 3-5 years ago. Trying to run modern 'state of the art' software systems on PCs that are ancient will generate frustration. Keep your equipment up-to-date and fit-for-purpose. The capital costs now are low.

A slow running system may be an indicator that a virus infection has taken place or that spy-ware is running secretly. It is always a good idea to have a security system (discussed earlier) installed that is kept up-to-date via on-line live updates from the suppliers. Many of these products also come with suites of computer maintenance facilities that could aid in some of the above steps.

Most advanced defragmenting like Diskeeper or PerfectDisk provide better disk clean up for a modest price compared to the free Windows ScanDisk. Another advanced tool is SpinRite which will confirm that all your data is correct on the hard disk.

Computer maintenance programs should be scheduled to run at least once a month. Some of these tasks, such as the virus scan and the security updates, can be set to run automatically over a weekend. Other tasks, such as removing programs, have to be done manually.

SUMMARY

Most of the technologies we discussed in this chapter are readily available to midsize and small businesses, and in fact, are being used in a variety of configurations today. The key for smaller businesses is to recognize the potential of these readily available technologies to help optimize their business operations and execute where feasible. At a minimum, there are those technologies that should be added to your "must have" list, that perhaps are being considered as nice to have, such as a UPS system and a shredder. The costs are relatively small when compared to the inherent value they bring to your business.

CHAPTER 3

MARKETING TECHNOLOGIES

Any business, big or small, is judged by its customers and potential customers on how it presents itself to the outside world. The public face your business displays to the world is part advertising, part communication, and all style. It is how you want your customer to think about you and how they actually think about, and remember, you. Certain business technology can enable you to communicate with and present yourself to customers and suppliers. For example, with the explosion of internet capabilities, there is now a completely new way to interact with customers, far flung employees and suppliers. This chapter describes the different technologies available to you, as a small business, and how you can use technology effectively to market your business beyond the traditional tools of the trade.

First let's break down marketing technologies into two segments based on what we want our communication to accomplish:

- Expanding the face of your business
- Evolving the relationship with your customers

The digital face that you portray on the Internet through your web page, social networking and blogs is a vital part of your overall on-line presence. Not only do you need to look good on the Internet and make yourself as visible as possible (just like your physical business location needs to look professional), but these new technologies are an incredible opportunity for new kinds of marketing and customer acquisition activities.

YOUR WEBSITE – THE HEART OF YOUR ON-LINE BUSINESS

A web site is now virtually mandatory for any business, however small. There are now hundreds of millions of potential customers worldwide who look to do business electronically through the Internet. Any business not taking this seriously in the 21st century is missing huge opportunities. Putting a basic web site on the net via an ISP is easy – many school kids of seven or eight (or even younger) have shown themselves perfectly capable of putting up a basic one or two page site. So the small business excuse of "it's too complicated" doesn't hold water! It is fair to say of course, that there are web sites and then again there are web sites.

Many businesses started out tentatively with a basic site with some banner advertising. This type of site may have just a few information-based pages with classic headings along the lines of "who are we" and "what do we do." Content on the site is usually limited to contact details for the company, a little of its history, and sometimes some frequently asked questions (FAQs). There is little a customer can do on this type of site other than finding some background information and sending an email enquiry. These "starter" websites have very limited functionality and may be perceived by customers as unprofessional.

To some extent that perception is valid, but starting like this does allow a company to experiment with basic web page building techniques. For simple pages and sites like this, most businesses should be quickly able to pick up the required skills or hire a web developer to get it done in a couple of days. Another advantage of starting small is that a business gets a presence on the Internet faster than if it waited for a full-blown e-commerce site. This can be important – business cards can carry that vital "WWW" address that is so important these days for advertising and for personal credibility. No matter how complex in terms of provided services your website becomes, you need to take the time to make your website attractive and compelling. How usable your site is will greatly affect whether or not potential customers will purchase something from your business. A Genex/Synovate survey found that 65% of Internet users will not shop from a poorly designed website. That is a lot of business to lose!

EXPANDING YOUR WEBSITE'S CAPABILITIES

One of the first capabilities that most small businesses add to their website after developing an initial basic site is the capability to view available products and services. Sometimes this is a simple affair that amounts to a page of images or text on the website that is updated daily or weekly based on inventory. However, more and more companies are providing an elaborate electronic "catalog" for their customers to browse. These on-line catalogs are updated automatically based on the business's inventory!

Setting up an on-line catalog can be quite challenging and takes a fair amount of time and work. But the payback can be enormous. Nothing helps sales like the customer being able to see an image and read a description of exactly what they are hoping to buy. The next step in complexity is to tie this on-line catalog into a full scale e-commerce solution where the customer can purchase the item on-line rather than calling your business and ordering over the phone. This means setting up order tracking and a system to deal with financial transactions.

A final topic needs to be mentioned here; web browser compatibility. There are a number of programs called web browsers that you can use to access the internet, made by a few different companies. The most well known one is Internet Explorer made by Microsoft. While every different type of web browser should display every web page the same way, different browsers may not show your site correctly (or at all!) if your website is not designed properly. As your website becomes more complex, you will have more and more of these "compatibility issues" to deal with.

YOUR WEBFRONT IS AS IMPORTANT AS YOUR STOREFRONT

Even if starting with a basic site, it is important to remember that the web site is a business portal for e-customers. Just like the business that is on a main street would not allow a shabby, amateurish window display of its goods, the web site, right at the outset, must create an appropriate professional impression and show that the company it represents has the right business environment. Paying a little extra to have quality graphics and content developed for your small business is worth the cost. Consider how your website looks as advertising – poorly designed advertising drives customers away instead of reeling them in.

WEB SITE ADVERTISING

Regardless of the type of web site a business has put onto the web, very often the initial excitement and anticipation quickly fades to disappointment as it suddenly discovers that no-one is visiting its site, let alone buying products through it. *You feel like you have paid for a huge billboard on a dead-end street.* To understand why this could happen, one has to consider one important difference between a virtual shop on the Internet and a physical shop in, for example, a mall. In a mall or main street shopping area, potential customers of the business will fall into one of two categories:

Category 1 - Those who know the business has a shop there and have come specifically to visit it and possibly purchase something.
Category 2 - Those who have "discovered" the shop in passing while looking around the shops in general.

To get any customers at all through a real shop, the business must open the shop in a place that is likely to get passing customer traffic. This gives them their "category 2" customers above. To get customers in through knowledge, the business has to advertise as well as rely on repeat customers and referrals from happy customers. In the case of an Internet shop, the same basic principles apply but how you go about them is different.

On the Internet, potential customers are sometimes referred to as "surfers" or "browsers." They are not unlike those people who go to a mall or shopping precinct for a look-around and may be attracted into a shop that catches their eye. The trouble is that the Internet is VAST! Imagine a mall the size of the whole planet. The chances of anybody casually finding your shop's Internet site in passing are small indeed. To attract the attention of potential new customers, the web site owners have to do something about it! As with any business, it is about how you market and your on-line business is no different.

ONLINE E-MALLS

FIGURE 3.1 eBay is one of the top providers of e-stores online

One option on the Internet is to place a shop or e-commerce

outlet in an electronic mall. In this case the company's web site is listed in a grouping of sites under the banner of the mall. The mall then advertises through various sources and tries to attract passing e-customers on the Internet in exactly the same way a real mall would, relying on the advertising that the "mall" does to bring business to your site.

This can often work well and provide the individual shops within the e-mall real benefit. Remember the mall will ask for subscription fees. And as a small business you will want to continue to brand you business independent of the e-store.

SEARCH OPTIMIZATION

The next marketing alternative is to exploit one of the strengths and weaknesses of the Internet – Search. When someone browses the Internet, even casually, they usually do so in part via search queries. They effectively ask the Internet to show them information on a topic such as "candle makers." In response, the search engine will shoot off all around the Internet looking for such information and typically will display links to tens if not hundreds of thousands of pages of information in response. These responses may include links to web sites on subjects that range across a history of candle making, French candle makers of the 15th century, scientific reports on the ingredients in scented candles, fire department safety advice on how to avoid candle created fires, and so on. The list will be of gargantuan proportions.

The person searching can refine their search to eliminate a lot of unwanted information by searching for "candle makers San Francisco" or "candle retailers in Richmond VA" but even so, the responses are still likely to number in the tens of thousands. This phenomenon is known as "information overload" – because nobody can possibly read and understand a significant percentage of these responses. Therefore the various Internet search engines use a technique called relevance ranking through mathematical algorithms.

When the search engine goes off to search, it uses programs that are called spiders or bots to search. These programs use the algorithm to rank in order of perceived relevance, those hits they find on the terms searched for. This is known as search optimization or search placement. The actual mathematics used by the search engines is complicated and involves many factors, but one thing is clear. If the candle company just puts their e-commerce web site on the Internet in the hope that someone keying in homemade candles into their browser will immediately see their e-shop, then they're very mistaken.

Internet browsers for the most part are subject to the same advertising psychology as conventional shoppers. If a search for "candle retailers" returns several hundred pages of information relating to 127,500 Internet hits with that phrase, then in general the browser and potential customer will perhaps read the first 1-3 pages only. If our candle company's web site is entry number 75,256 on page number 274 of the search then they can be sure that no potential customer will ever read that far to spot it. In other words the placement is wrong.

Source: www.google.com - Copyright © 2009 Google, Inc. All rights reserved.

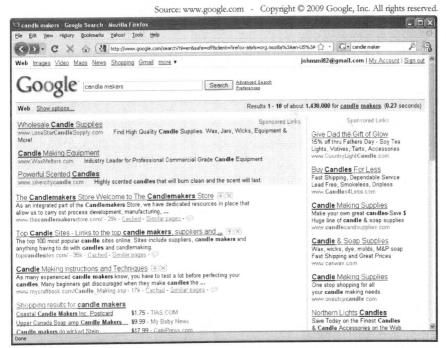

FIGURE 3.2 Google is the undisputed leader of search engines

As a business owner, you need to understand the general issues behind internet searching. However there are consulting firms who can make sure that your website will show up at the top of search lists for any relevant search words. It is worth the reasonably small investment to pay one of these companies for this service. Businesses should remember – however good the site is technically and conceptually, it will be useless if people do not know it is there!

BUSINESS & SOCIAL NETWORKING

People have always had to achieve certain things to survive in business: improving their visibility, showcasing their talents and advertising their products and services are some of them. Businesses have also needed to "network," maintain a visibility and engage with their peer group. Much as we like to believe that modern society rewards based on merits, the age-old saying "it's not what you know but rather who you know that counts" is very much rooted in reality. As such, business people have always turned to available technology to help them communicate and be visible. Whether it was a wax tablet, a parchment scroll, the billboards of the 19th century or now the Internet, the basic need has remained unchanged.

For many years the Internet was exploited in this fashion in a rather crude way. The junk/spam email was the best many could come up with as electronic advertising. To their credit, many small businesses understood early on the importance of Internet advertising through other on-line sites and effective search optimization techniques.

Nowadays, businesses should consider certain types of websites that are dedicated to networking (of the personal and professional type) and showcasing – in other words telling everyone that cares to look, exactly who you are and what you're good at. There are sites on the Internet that are dedicated to these very functions and they make it easy for a business to gain visibility and market penetration. There is a fairly widespread misconception in some business circles that some of these sites are dedicated to amusement and adolescents. This is a mistake and a possible lost opportunity.

Social networking is a useful platform for contact and proliferating awareness of an individual and/or company. Some of these sites have their origins in things such as high-school associations or hobby groups and to some extent they still carry some reputation baggage as a result. Now, they are playing an increasing part in business activities. Social network sites such as Facebook and MySpace, blog sites and video and photo sharing portals, though generally started as simple social venues, have exploded into vast on-line communities that are just like any other city. They share, they communicate… and they buy. It is important to remember that social networking is not pure advertising as such but rather a form of linked communication that may, and often does, result in a form of advertising. In some of these social networking sites, it is possible to upload photographs of individuals and update their professional history. This person can be linked to others and perhaps other companies they know. These are professional networks that can be used to highlight current web sites and even load videos that can be browsed by others and show details of products or premises.

There is a wealth of possibilities in the way you can interact with your customers using social networking. You can keep existing customers updated with a Facebook page; send daily specials via Twitter; provide value added content and support through a blog; or simply advertise your business on MySpace. Let's take a look at some of these possibilities in detail.

CREATING AN ON-LINE COMMUNITY

Think of social networking sites as one big community hall that can seat millions. Everybody is talking with everybody else about every topic under the sun – and it is the people who are most interesting or who are talking about a topic that is interesting who have the largest group of people to talk to. Using social networking for business is about becoming that interesting "person" in the crowd. Social networking is not standard advertising. Generally you are not there to hype your products and services. The social networking presence of your business should be informative and interesting and be about your particular field of business. Just like any interesting conversationalist, however, you should also be able to talk about many different topics as well. This is what will bring in people who normally would not be aware of your business.

This is the key to social advertising – you are putting a personal face on your business that will seem to act in a very individual way. Your business can grab people's attention by talking to them almost one on one. There are a number of different ways that you can provide this individual sort of presence. Having accounts on the most popular social networking sites is a good start. But you need to go beyond that – just being there isn't enough. Social networking is an ongoing activity – you have to make your business a valuable part of the community by being active in that community with updates, conversations, advice and entertainment.

The most common ways to develop "social content" is to provide advice and reviews for both your products and your particular industry. Another way is to write a regular blog about your business area. Many businesses have their employees blog about being part of its business and give advice. You do have to be careful with social networking – it is not moderated but it is remembered. This means that everything you say in your blogs or on your social networking sites, good or bad, will be recorded forever. An inadvertent and careless remark made by an employee or employer can be picked up by others at a speed that is almost unimaginable. It is the business that is always helping out the community, providing free advice, being generally helpful, and being just plain fun that is the business that will be talked about by others and recommended. The social networking community is no different. It is that word of mouth advertising that is the ultimate point of making your business part of a social network.

SOCIAL NETWORK MARKETING

As we previously discussed, you can use social networking to plug your products and services, but this has to be done in a balanced way. If all you do is hawk your own business on the social sites, you will end up with no one who will stay with the site. You will lose the biggest gain of social networking – bringing in friends of friends and random people who happened to notice something about one of your postings. Keep your postings about your own products and services brief and to the point. Don't be afraid to provide links to external reviews – both good and bad. The most effective way to advertise with social networking is to simply make people aware of what you are selling – then let your reputation within the community do the actual advertising for you.

However, let's not forget that social networks are also an excellent starting point for regular advertising as well. Sites such as Facebook display ads on almost every single page that a user clicks on. More importantly, ads are targeted to audiences depending on the profiles of each user. By advertising on a social networking site, you can target your ads to a specific group. You can also tie your ads to your social networking site as well. Again, this has to be done with a bit of caution – if you inundate your potential customers with regular advertising, they will start to feel as though you are always trying to sell something with your social networking contacts, even when you are simply being genuinely helpful.

POPULAR SOCIAL NETWORKING SITES

There are many sites of this nature including Twitter, Facebook, LinkedIn, MySpace and even YouTube. Each site has its own style and the type of information it was originally designed to share amongst its community. That means that each site will provide different opportunities to the smaller business in terms of customer relationships and advertising.

FACEBOOK

Facebook has its origin in the concept of helping friends keep in touch. It is based on the idea that individuals can create a page on the site dedicated to themselves and their interests. They can then link into that page all the contact details for their friends on the same site. This means that if they changed anything about their page, their friends would automatically be able to see what had changed and pass this onto their friends in turn. This may sound slightly trivial and not a serious business subject, but it would be wise to pause for a second and think about it.

FIGURE 3.3 A Facebook page is an excellent tool for interacting with customers

How many businesses have, from time to time, wondered about how they can inform their customers of a change in their business operations? Perhaps they have just moved to a new and more prestigious business address and would like to make that as widely known as possible? Alternatively, a business may have just launched a new product and would like to bring this to the attention of its customers? Many businesses, big and small, are now setting themselves up with a Facebook page and creating a social network of their contacts/fans around it. Yes, it is true that these business contacts need to be using Facebook, but it is a rapidly growing environment that already has over 150 million global users – this is a vast marketplace potential.

So how would a small business actually use Facebook? At a basic level, Facebook can be used to place advertisements. These advertisements can be defined to be specifically visible only to certain market segments – such as males in the USA between the ages of 18 and 25. Yet this is just scratching the surface. By constructing the business page to show news feeds such as "new special offers available", everyone on the business page's network will get automatic notification of the change.

FIGURE 3.4 Businesses use Facebook to acquire and retain customers

In a sense, it is like free update advertising in more or less real time. Everyone so connected will have the opportunity to see that the company has just released a new product and hopefully click on the link to have a look-see. In addition these business pages can also allow people to directly link to a company's own main website. It is probably correct to say that Facebook is still in the early stages of its development as a major business tool. But Facebook recognizes the possibilities for businesses and has been rapidly creating services specifically designed for the business market. This is exactly the right time to get on board.

LINKEDIN

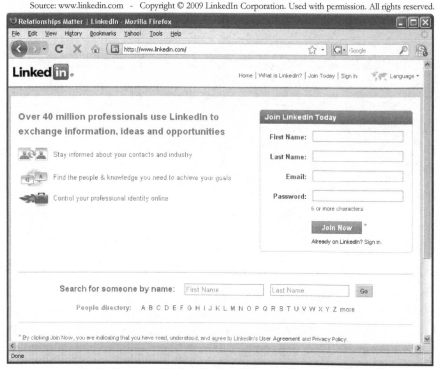

FIGURE 3.5 LinkedIn is the premier platform for business networking

LinkedIn does for professionals what Facebook does for friends and social groups – keeps acquaintances and associates updated on each other's professional lives. A good way to think of LinkedIn is a business club, where conversations and contacts are as much about business as they are about developing personal interactions. At its core, LinkedIn is about professionals being able to maintain a list of contact details for people (called "connections") that they are potentially interested in doing business with – sort of like an on-line rolodex. The difference here is that you also can see who other people in your list are connected to – just like being able to see their rolodex.

LinkedIn is particularly useful for driving business to business sales, but again it is not through traditional advertising. You don't walk into a business club and start handing out flyers. You walk in, join the club, and start getting to know other members well. Soon people you know will introduce you to others who they know that may be potential customers. Alternatively you can ask a connection for an introduction to one of their connections. The site also provides a service called "Answers" where users can post questions to be answered by anyone else who is a member of LinkedIn. Providing useful advice in a forum like this shows not only your professionalism and knowledge, but will help to portray your business as being approachable and helpful. Let's use a Realtor Company as an example. One of the agents at the company has set herself up with a LinkedIn account. One day she notices a question posted on the site asking for information on how land prices have changed over the years in the area of the city where she works.

Our Realtor agent spends a minute to check some historical prices on the company's database, then posts a quick and succinct response to the question giving the general range in prices over the last five years. As it happens, a developer from the same city also saw the question on the site, as well as the answer. Recognizing the agent's knowledge and expertise, the developer contacts the agent through her LinkedIn profile, and arranges to set up a meeting to discuss potential sites for his new development. In this very common example, our small business used no advertising – and yet was still able to generate new business. This is the power of social networking. This point can't be stressed enough – you join LinkedIn to provide advice and become a respected member of the club. Sales will come from acquaintances who will recommend you to others who are looking for the particular goods or services that you sell.

MYSPACE

MySpace is a social networking site geared to the younger (30 and under) demographic. More than Facebook, MySpace is about allowing individuals to create a homepage that they can show off to their friends. As part of this, MySpace is built towards allowing users to provide music and videos on their homepages that they can share with their friends and other people who browse their MySpace page. So MySpace is going to be particularly useful for a small business that is related to the music industry or movie industry, especially independent movies and bands.

Designed by Brandon Weiss,
Music Industry Program, Class of 2009.

FIGURE 3.6 Businesses of all sizes creatively leverage their MySpace pages

For other small businesses, MySpace now offers an advertising service, called MyAds, which allows you to place ads that are targeted for specific regions, specific types of people, or both. Suppose you are the owner of a small used CD and independent artist CD shop in Seattle. You decide to set up a MySpace page, which provides basic information about your store and link as friends any local bands that are from the Seattle area. Every day, you upload a new song track from a CD you have available in your store. You also write short reviews on various local bands and post them onto your MySpace page. To get more people aware of your site, you then use the MyAds facility to post an ad about your store to people using MySpace who are 40 and younger and who live in Seattle. These people can click on the ad, which will point them to your MySpace page and also to your own business website.

MySpace does tend to be more advertisement focused than other social networking sites – which on first glance seems better for the small business. However, the demographic is more limited than other sites, and may not be the most suitable for your business's products or services.

TWITTER

Twitter is described as a micro-blogging service. What that means is that people can post brief comments no longer than 140 characters at a time, called tweets. Other people can choose to "follow" that person (or business), reading those tweets as they are posted. Earlier it seems as though Twitter could have no valuable use for a business – and certainly the service was initially designed so that friends could keep each other updated on their lives in almost real time.

But twitter has become popular enough that many people are now following each other's lives and businesses. If social networking is a community hall, think of Twitter as the BBQ out back during the meeting. Twitter is about light, social conversation that can tie a community together by keeping everybody aware of current events and gossip.

How can this sort of thing help a small business? Again, it is the idea of popularity and building long term contacts. People who find you interesting will start to follow your tweets. In fact, people can see just how many other people have chosen to follow your feed. For businesses, it most definitely is NOT about advertising. In fact, many Twitterers are very put off by businesses that advertise using Twitter. What businesses can do, however, is be at that BBQ. Businesses can talk shop, share stories with people and give advice.

FIGURE 3.7 WholeFoods tweets with over 1 million followers

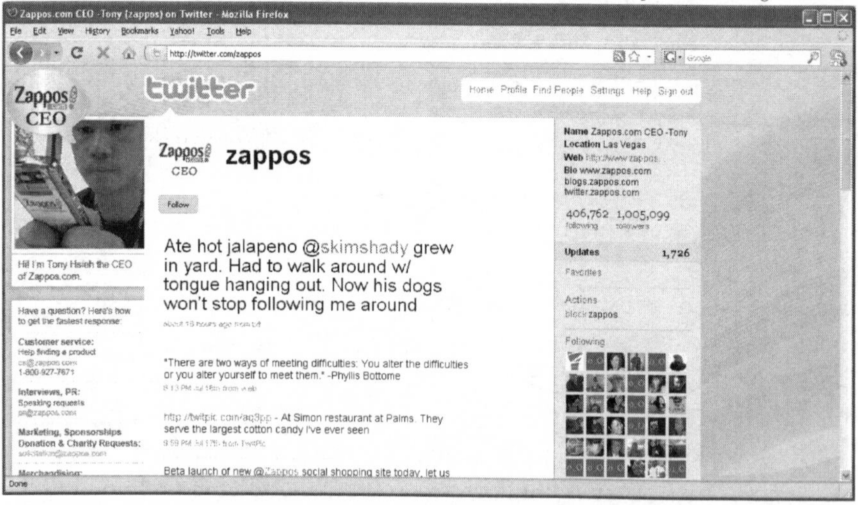

FIGURE 3.8 Zappos CEO has over 1 million following his tweets

For example, WholeFoods hold interactive conversations with customers, answering questions and taking suggestions. Zappos, the on-line clothing company, uses twitter to build their brand by providing advice and information and answering tweets that others have posted. Twitter is about building long term relationships that will drive long term sales through word of mouth. As a business, it is an excellent way to plug into networks of people around the globe who have similar interests and who potentially provide large amounts of word of mouth advertising.

YOUTUBE ™

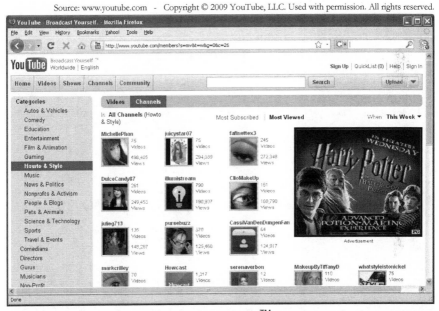

FIGURE 3.9 Savvy entrepreneurs use YouTube™ to connect with clients

This web site is regularly accessed by millions of people worldwide and has become something of a global phenomenon. YouTube allows people to upload their videos for anyone to watch across the Internet. The videos can be grouped together by subject matter or by owner and these groupings are often called a channel. For some time YouTube had the reputation of being an environment for hobbyists and adolescents – but this is now history. YouTube is now being used increasingly by businesses to advertise their products and services. There are now special offerings and sections for business advertising and business channels. These can even be linked to other areas of the YouTube site to enhance their visibility. This of course begs the question, "What can one upload?"

Well, almost anything. Let's take a candle making business as an example. The company could upload a series of videos under their own channel name. One of these may be a brief walk around the premises which could convey an image of reliability to potential buyers. A second video might take potential buyers on a quick tour of the inside of their premises for the same reasons.

Perhaps another video on the channel could show buyers exactly how the candles are manufactured. Then perhaps a final video could contain a message from the business owner about their values and customer service principles. It is even possible to link these channels and ads directly to a themed search. Let's say someone browsing YouTube searches on "aroma therapy." Although not immediately a candle subject, that person's search may indicate that they'd have a potential interest in scented candles. So the candle business's channel could be made visible at that time to catch their eye.

FIGURE 3.10 YouTube provides an excellent platform for marketing products

A company selling specialized used cars could have a video showing each vehicle externally and internally. Another video could show the engine running. With moving images, one can communicate much more than with a simple written ad. The possibilities are almost endless. In general, YouTube is an excellent advertising and communication forum and its global reach offers smaller businesses huge opportunities for expansion and international exposure.

BUSINESS NETWORKING & SHOWCASING THROUGH BLOGS

Source: www.fromnaturewithlove.com - © 2009 Natural Sourcing, LLC. Used with permission. All rights reserved.

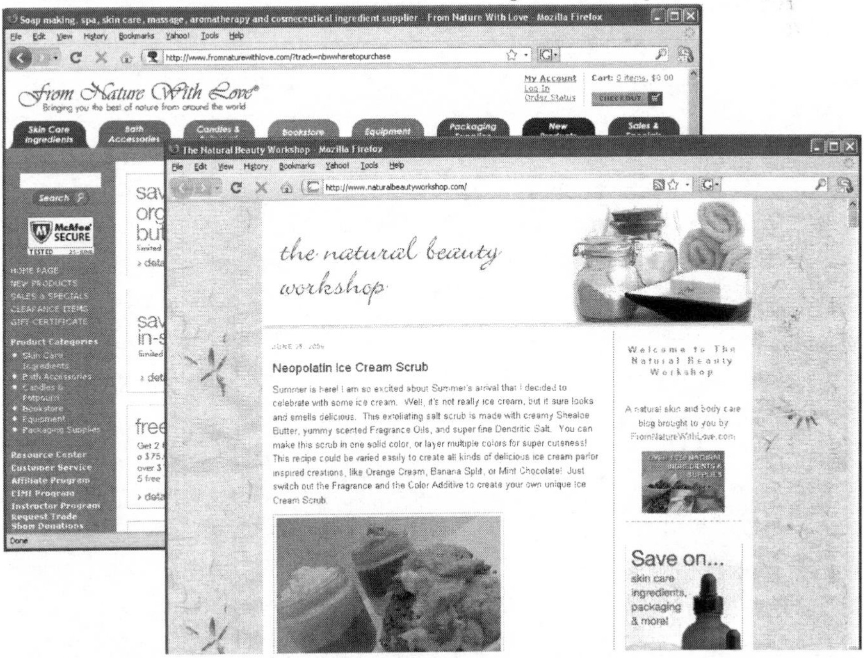

FIGURE 3.11 A well written blog can add tremendous value to a business site

If a business is using websites such as YouTube or Facebook, then they are already aware of the growing power of the Internet as a channel for advertising and business engagement. As a result, they also probably have two overriding objectives 1) to achieve the maximum visibility of their website in internet searches and 2) to drive traffic to their website. There is little point ensuring the visibility of a business's web site in searches if, having seen it, nobody decides to go and have a look. There are several ways to overcome this potential lack of appeal and one of the more popular is the blog. Many web sites have a section called "blogs."

A blog is a short, informally written piece (typically around 500-750 words) on a subject. Blogs have their origin in people's personal diaries. Somebody would simply write up what they'd done that particular day or perhaps just share their thoughts on a given subject. They would then publish this on the Internet for anyone interested to read.

The business potential of a blog became quickly apparent to some technology savvy businesses. Because a blog can be titled and written on any subject, it is a good way of attracting "passing traffic" to a given web site. Let's consider an example that relates to our candle making business. Perhaps at a given time there is a lot of media attention on a major national event such as a presidential inauguration or the opening of a major art gallery. Although neither of these is directly related to candle making, the owner of the candle web site could write a quick blog on presidential inaugurations or art galleries just stating their perceptions and observations. Later, someone who sees the blog's entry when scanning an internet search on "Presidential inaugurations" may perhaps click onto the candle site to read the blog.

It's not unusual to see web sites with blog sections that are full of posts that seemingly have little relationship to the main web site's purpose. Now the reason is clear! They do so to drive casual traffic to the site. There is no doubt that the Internet will continue to grow and diversify as a commercial marketplace and at a phenomenal rate in the years ahead. Blogging is currently getting a lot of small business attention and will receive even more in the immediate future. This is the time to start to explore the potential!

STARTING YOUR OWN BLOG

The key to a good blog is the same as for any successful writing: it must be entertaining and informative. No one is going to read your business blog if it is dull or if it only talks about the stock order purchase you made last Monday. You can set up your blog on your own website, and this is easiest to do using blogging tools such as WordPress. These software packages allow you to write up your blogs and post them to your website through your service provider. They are normally very simple to use. Another option that many small businesses choose is to use one of the many blogging sites such as Blogspot, Blogger or LiveJournal. In the profile on your blog site, you can provide a link back to your business website. The advantage of going this route is that the blogging site provides all the tools you need to quickly set up and start writing a blog without needing to make any changes to your own website.

Ideally, either you or one of your employees would write the company blog. But not everyone has writing skills; fortunately there are many freelance writers out there who will write and update your blog for you. In this case, you can either provide possible stories and ideas, or ask the writer to come up with ideas for you. Whether you are writing the blog yourself, or having someone write it for you, the key is to provide *constant, fresh* content. That means updating the blog at least a few times a week with new posts. The most popular blogs are those that people can reliably check on a daily basis to provide a brief moment of entertainment. While you are entertaining people each time they read your blog – even when the blogs are not business topics – the readers are remembering that your business exists. That is the key to a successful business blog.

SUMMARY

In this age of instant communication, maintaining a solid and reliable image of your company to the outside world is even more important than ever. Luckily, there is a whole new range of technologies to help maintain that positive image, acquiring new customers and retaining existing ones in the process. Whether it is blogging for old or prospective clients, posting advice to potential clients via LinkedIn, or tweeting about daily giveaways or sales, technology is providing the means to help you keep your customers informed about your business and you informed about your customers.

CHAPTER 4

CUSTOMER & SUPPLIER INTERACTION TECHNOLOGIES

This chapter describes the different technologies available to you as a midsize or small business, to effectively interact with and learn about your customers and suppliers. It focuses on customer and supplier engagement, outlining how you can use technology to not only keep track of customers and suppliers, but also how you can use technology to gain valuable insights and significantly strengthen the relationships.

VIDEO CONFERENCING

Today more than ever, almost every business, small and large needs to keep extremely tight control over its costs. Business travel can be a major cost to the small business. It is not just the actual cost of plane or train fare, but also the time lost in between flights (though with today's Smartphone and wireless laptops we can be somewhat productive), the cost of rental cars, hotel accommodations, and entertainment. The time lost in travel is a huge 'opportunity cost' that many businesses fail to take account of. Every minute spent stuck in traffic, waiting for a late train, or fuming in an airport over a cancelled flight, is costing your business. It doesn't matter whether you're using planes, trains, or automobiles; travel is expensive.

Anyone who has traveled regularly on business also knows from experience that the amount of time spent with the person at destination is frequently only a small percentage of the time invested in the meeting. If it takes 2 hours to get to a meeting that lasts 45 minutes, then including return journeys means that 4 hours business time and cost have been invested for only 45 minutes potentially productive activity. The environmental effects of mass travel are also becoming more and more of a political and economic issue. As a result businesses, large and small, are looking to play their part in reducing their carbon footprint.

FIGURE 4.1 Video conferencing is now common place in businesses

For all these reasons, most businesses today are trying to reduce or eliminate much of their travel needs. They are increasingly turning to conferencing technologies to help them achieve that. The idea of 'distance conferencing' via technology is far from new. For at least half a century, it has been possible to link multiple parties together on a phone system allowing people in several locations to 'join in' a single telephone conference or 'telecon' as it became known. In the 1970s and 1980s many meeting rooms acquired the conference box or pod that sat in the middle of the table and allowed all participants to speak to others in several different locations. This technology still exists today. It remains widely used and it generally works well. Various locations can be linked together via dedicated lines or more commonly, through a telephone operator conferencing system.

FIGURE 4.2 Very robust web-based conferencing tools are now readily available

Numerous conference sites on the Internet offer a more modern digital version of the classic teleconferencing systems. These offer PC users the opportunity to connect into the conferencing site over the Internet from their office PC or even a mobile phone. Various offices in multiple locations can join in a single discussion with the participants speaking through their PC's microphone without needing to leave their desk. Some companies offer these conferencing facilities free-of-charge or at a very low cost.

However, as useful as the telecon is, it suffers from two drawbacks. The first of these is: when multiple people are connected in more than two locations, the meeting can degenerate into chaos if everyone tries to speak at the same time. To avoid this, some form of structure and chairing is required for the meeting, which can inhibit free-flowing conversation and exchange of ideas. The second problem arises from the fact that the parties involved cannot see each other. This is important and relates to some of the face-to-face issues touched on at the outset of this section. In some situations, particularly if the parties are strangers to each other and/or originate from different countries and cultures, verbal communication can be problematic. What may sound on the phone like sarcasm, ridicule, negativism or even downright rudeness, may be interpreted differently if the speaker's facial and body language could be seen.

This is where video conferencing can make a big difference while helping to cut down significantly on the amount of traveling required. Video conferencing sometimes carries a little baggage with it in terms of its reputation. It has also been around for some decades and available with excellent quality. In the 1980s and the 1990s that good quality was only obtainable in very expensive systems and accessible only to big businesses, usually involving dedicated high-speed communication lines between locations. The early Internet and video phone solutions available to small business were by contrast much less impressive. Picture freezes, jerky images, voice and image out-of-synch characterized this technology then. It may have been relatively low cost, but it just wasn't suitable for business communications and conferencing.

Today this is all history. It is now possible to achieve extremely good quality videoconferencing through your PC to another PC anywhere in the world. This is called point-to-point conferencing and usually involves a party at one location speaking to another party at a second location. All you need is a modern PC with a reasonable amount of memory, a good high-resolution screen, a desktop camera, and a high-speed connection to the Internet. In fact, virtually everything you need to achieve good point-to-point videoconferencing now comes as available options with most PCs and laptops, including the camera. This will become the standard in the coming few years. The advances in this technology over recent years may well allow you to eliminate much travel associated with those relatively informal 1-to-1 meetings that are so commonplace.

Some videoconferencing needs are slightly more demanding, involving multiple people and locations and the presentation of materials and graphics. In general, if your business engages regularly in this type of complex and formal conferencing, you may need a slightly more sophisticated solution including possibly a larger and more powerful screen and desktop box. There are numerous Internet companies that will both sell (or rent) this type of more specialized equipment and provide the Internet links to support multiple parties in this type of conference. In addition, and perhaps more optimal to the midsize and small business, are those internet companies that provide full scale conferencing solutions on an as needed basis.

There are several well known companies out there. They offer solutions that can meet the needs of any midsize or small business from the individual working on a single PC right up to large business operating across multiple locations. Their system allows someone to click on an icon and instantly connect to someone else. Both parties can see each other in a corner of the screen. The benefits can be huge for a small business that typically requires much travel and face time with clients/customers.

When considering a move to videoconferencing, it is important to understand fully your likely usage and requirements before going out and buying or renting equipment. The costs have fallen significantly in recent years, but it is probably worthwhile to take some professional advice beforehand.

COLLABORATION

Regardless of a business's size, there is increasing emphasis on shared creations and discoveries, tapping into the collective talent existing within businesses or industries. No longer is it acceptable to keep an idea to yourself for fear of it being co-opted by another team member. Current thinking is that with different lenses focused on an idea, it can only get better, faster. As a result many businesses look to more efficiently utilize the skills and expertise of their employees and partners via collaborative techniques and tools. This is the convergence of individuals and groups from various backgrounds, locations and disciplines working together in virtual teams on a common objective. This move towards formal collaborative activities is also being driven by changes in the business environment, with businesses needing to find ways of creating better products faster.

Collaboration is, of course, not new and has been achieved historically within and between companies. A shared business goal or process may get needed contributions from various centres of excellence such as Accounting, Sales and Manufacturing and perhaps an external supplier. Some of these groups may physically reside in different locations, including individuals working primarily from home. Co-ordinating and rationalizing the differences in skills, backgrounds, styles, expectations and people towards that common objective has been a big part of project management requiring a lot of manual effort.

Even so, however gifted a project manager, there were traditionally a number of obstacles to efficiently setting up and controlling shared collaborative activities. At one time, simple collaboration was restricted to the distribution of a copy of a project plan and the demand that people record their progress directly against it. This tended to be random and usually failed to integrate into other elements of the collaboration tasks. Many common "shared directories" on computer networks were widely ignored because of this.

Even in the best-run business, the lack of visibility and tight systematic controls meant that much work collaboration remained fairly loose and the outputs scattered and varied. Fortunately, the situation has evolved for the better and a new generation of technology products are around that provide an excellent environment for facilitating and managing true collaborative activities. Examples of this type of system would include Microsoft's Sharepoint, Huddle, or CentralDesktop.

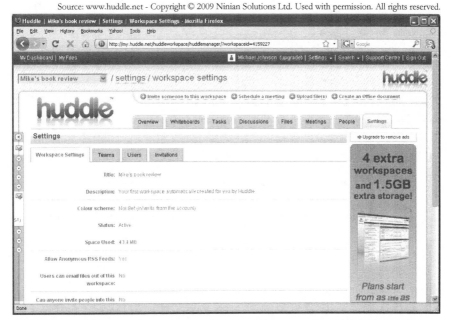

FIGURE 4.3 Online collaboration makes it easy for businesses to get started

These tools share certain characteristics. Groups of people can have common work areas where all activities are recorded and stored. Teams wanting to collaborate on an idea can work within a single work area focused on a single combined output. The software helps to control access and allows assigned individuals to work on a single product from multiple locations. All the related documents are defined and visible to all who need to see and access it, with check-out, check-in, and versioning. If someone makes a change to (e.g.) a collectively developed presentation, everyone within that collaborative team can be notified of the change and all can provide input for all to see.

As everything is stored and indexed centrally, this significantly reduces the risks of key pieces of the combined effort being 'lost' and unavailable should a single staff member be off sick, etc. This type of technology allows activities and outputs to be linked to a project plan of sorts with deadlines. Responsibilities in terms of contributing towards an activity are allocated, recorded, distributed and tracked. Reminders are built into the calendar and communicated automatically.

On-line conferencing (including video where possible) both from within the business location as well as with external parties can also be facilitated. One of the more mundane tasks associated with collaborative activities is simply keeping tabs on who is working on what activity, where they are based, their skill sets and contact details. Modern collaboration technology will keep and make available centrally all such information.

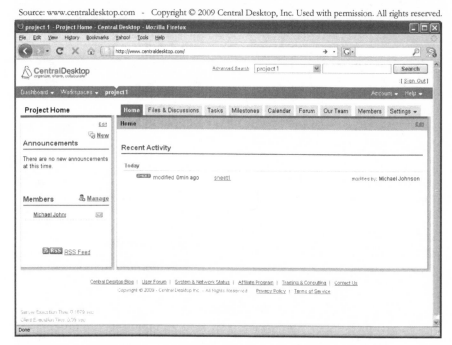

FIGURE 4.4 Collaboration tools generally share some similar features

While the application of collaboration technologies in small business has not yet taken off it is clearly a technology that those businesses that require collaboration as a way of doing business or as a means to forge and build new partnerships, should follow closely. Huddle.net was used in my collaborative activities in the development of this book. One master document was used. All my reviewers were able to collectively make comments and provide input. One of the best results came from the fact that everyone was able to see what everyone else was doing and the quality of review and feedback on this book was tremendous.

CUSTOMER RELATIONSHIP MANAGEMENT (CRM)

Once upon a time, CRM was fairly simple. All that was needed to retain accounts was to give customers good service when they asked for it, plus the occasional business lunch. Today it's considerably more complex. Both the customer and the business have changed their views of what CRM should entail.

From the business's point of view, customer service is, of course, still of paramount importance. If you cannot get the customer what they want, when they want it and supported by decent customer service, then you won't need to worry about CRM because you'll very quickly have no customers left. Savvy businesses now want *to understand* their customers in total.

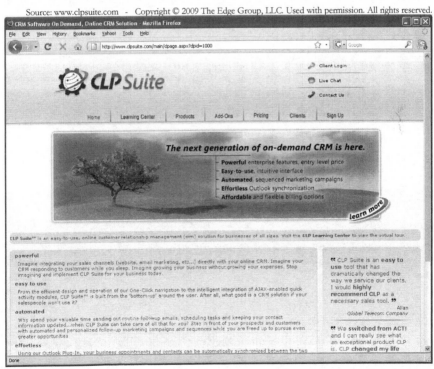

FIGURE 4.5 Much anticipated online CRM tools are now available

- *What are their relationships to other clients?* Shortly after sending out that 'hard line' letter to a customer is not the time to discover that one of their parents is your biggest and most valued account.

- *How profitable is their business?* In some industries 80% of the company's profits can come from only 10-15% of their customer base. You'll want to know where your customer sits in that spectrum as part of your customer servicing and decision making processes.

- *What is their family situation?* Sending mail to people who are deceased or addressed to couples that have been divorced for years, can be distressing and reputation-ruining. You also need to know what will appeal to them and what is less likely to.

- *What are they buying from you?* This may sound easy but the same customer can purchase various goods under different names for perfectly legitimate reasons – e.g. personal and corporate purchasing.

- *Who and where are they?* Linked to the above point, it is important to understand whether two Mr. Smiths at the same address are in fact the same person. Are Mrs. L. Smith and Ms L. Jones at the same address two different people or is one usage the single name for professional reasons? Is Mr. Grant at one address the same person as Mr. Grant at a different address (e.g. personal and business address)?

- *What's their history with you?* Have there been disputes or complaints previously?

The list of questions could continue depending on the needs of a business. You need to know these things to:

1. Improve customer service and decision making
2. Avoid making blatant errors that damage your reputation and cause you to -lose accounts
3. Deploy your sales staff where they are most likely to yield increased results – i.e. with your most profitable customers

and customer segments
4. Possibly help 'manage-out' unprofitable customers
5. Develop targeted marketing propositions based on customer intelligence
6. Comply with legislation such as data protection and avoid the accidental disclosure of confidential information, etc.

From the customer's position, the requirements of a good relationship are evolving similarly. No customer today wishes to be treated like a complete stranger or 'first-time' customer every time they call a supplier. This isn't just a question of having someone greet them with "Hi, my name is Bill!" at the opening of a call. They want 'Bill' to be able to see immediately who they are from a simple name or reference *and* the totality of their dealings with the company. *"Do you have an account with us?"* *"Sorry, I have no record of your problem as here in accounts we can't see those details on our screen."* *"I can only see your payments not your outstanding orders."* Phrases like these are no longer acceptable. Customers now demand partnership from their suppliers rather than plain compliance. They want to receive offers and opportunities that are targeted specifically at them and their way of working, based upon what their supplier already knows of their transaction history. If they're purchasing wholesale quantities of organic food from you, they may see the logic of receiving a proposition relating to various forms of organic ice cream offers. They will probably be less amused to receive a phone call offering discounts on non-organic products.

For a business to develop an understanding of its customer base, it takes time and the help of a CRM system. It's important to understand that CRM systems are both technology as well as a set of disciplines and methodology. Any organization purchasing CRM will get rewards out of it that are directly proportional to the effort they invest in making it a success. Just purchasing CRM software and connecting it to the business's old systems will not necessarily deliver much, unless those systems are already extremely well structured and prepared for integrated customer management.

To implement such a system usually involves three separate activities. The first of these is to access all of the information available within a company that relates to 'the customer'. A CRM system cannot function effectively if only 50% of customer information is available. Getting information may involve building information feeds from existing customer databases, accounts systems, order processing systems, marketing systems, and complaints procedure systems and so on.

FIGURE 4.6 Advances in CRM technology optimizes workforce mobility

Next, the business needs to apply various processes to the data in order to interpret it. This may be a demanding task for larger organizations that have a large existing investment in disparate (i.e. not integrated) systems such as various lines of business systems and accounts. There may be a need for some significant data analysis. Most CRM systems come with powerful de-duplication engines that are able to merge customer information from various source systems according to business rules the business determines, so that a single integrated view is obtained. These rules come partly standardized as part of most CRM solutions, but they are also modified/enhanced and new ones created to handle specific business needs. The CRM system is then configured to merge and consolidate the various customer data once the above has been completed. A CRM system is not psychic, and it will not be able to tell automatically that Mrs. Lopez at address 1 is the same person as Mrs. Lopez at Déco Designs at a different business address. It will also not be able to work out for itself that Mrs. Reynolds is the daughter of the CEO of your most profitable client. Only the business, based on its interactions with each customer, can supply the information (assuming they know!) to make that possible. What CRM *can* do is provide you with the facility to reflect those relationships and knowledge, so that it is more widely available for use and awareness. You may not wish to merge the two Mrs. Lopez accounts into one client view. But it is unlikely that any company would not be interested in being able to *see* on their screens automatically, when looking at one account, that the other account also exists.

The final stage is for CRM systems to consolidate this customer information into a series of integrated views to allow a true customer intelligence approach to future business. At a glance, it should be possible to see the totality of the customer and their relationships with your organization. This information can potentially be made available to all appropriate personnel in the company to aid their individual communications with the client. Some companies make portions of this consolidated view accessible to their customers over the Internet. The various composite views and analysis presented by CRM systems is also of key use to marketing and development. They can see exactly what may or may not interest an existing client and how much time they should spend servicing and developing the account. For many years the slogan uttered in many companies has been: "Know the customer". Via CRM systems and methodologies, this is now becoming absolutely possible.

SUMMARY

The way we interact and engage current and prospective customers and suppliers is extremely important for the growth of the business. Customers can be loyal, but can easily jump to the next business if they do not feel well treated or respected. Technology, as we've seen, has provided us with some power tools to ensure that our customer interaction is topnotch. Failure to tap into them, at least before your competition does, is a great way of ensuring that they jump ship sooner rather than later.

Much of the technology has been around for quite some time, and large companies have spent millions implementing these tools to optimize customer and supplier engagement. All of those tools have been adapted and are now available to the midsize and small business at decent prices. It is clear that to succeed in the current and future business environment these technologies must be seriously considered by any business wishing to *grow*, or even *maintain* their customer base.

CHAPTER 5

BUSINESS EFFICIENCY TECHNOLOGIES

R emember that all technology processes must be seen and understood in business equivalent terms. Let's take a good look at how technology increases business efficiency and effectiveness, reducing or even eliminating wasted time in your day to day business activities. The technologies we refer to in this chapter are not the technologies that your customer normally sees you use. It is the technology that you should be using every day in your office and at your desk to actually run the day to day and longer term activities for your business.

The key to technology improving efficiency in the business is making sure you get and use the right technology for the right opportunity. For our discussion, we can divide those technologies that improve efficiency into three categories:

- Business information technologies
- Business operation technologies
- Business finance technologies

Every business, no matter how small, can use technology to increase efficiency in all three areas – but not every business will need every technology. Remember that the technology requirements of each business are unique because the efficiency requirements of each business are unique. It's time to look at the technologies that are available to increase business efficiency and effectiveness, starting with business information technologies.

BUSINESS INFORMATION TECHNOLOGIES

DATA BACKUP AND STORAGE

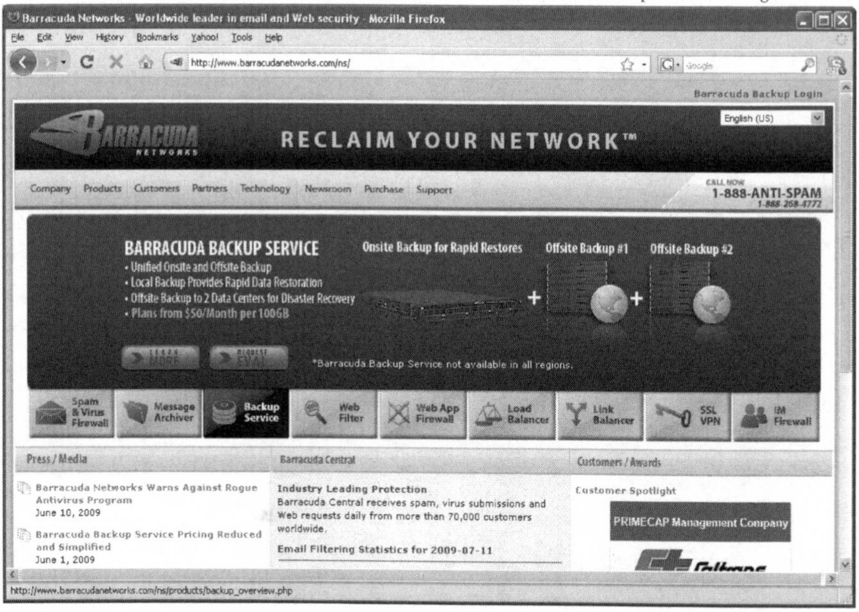

FIGURE 5.1 Backup tools have evolved and many are web-based

It doesn't matter how careful you are or even how lucky you think you are – sooner or later you're going to have a 'crash' of some sort on your business technology systems. Although modern technology is extremely robust and reliable compared to the standards of even 10-15 years ago, it still goes awry from time to time when pieces of hardware or software fail. In addition, it doesn't matter how reliable your technology is, it's a certainty that someone, at sometime, is going to do something careless with it. That cup of coffee that's just been spilled onto an open laptop, the PC system unit that's just been dropped from a desk as somebody tried to move it, the guy that's just drilled through your main network cable or the employee that has just accidentally deleted a set of master files – any one of these can cause your technology to grind to a halt and your business with it. Shortly after one of these events happens is not the time to start thinking about whether or not to invest in backups and recovery systems. Backing up your data is perhaps one of the most important yet overlooked activities for most business users. So what are the risks and what can be done about them?

The Risks

1) Many of the smallest companies are entirely reliant upon their information technology. If an entire system or even part of a system is unavailable, the business cannot function. The longer this remains the case, the greater chance that customers will lose patience and simply go elsewhere.

2) Even if the core technology is working, it may be next to useless if the basic data it needs to function is lost, corrupted or out-of-date. As an example, customers are not likely to find it funny that their last 5 orders have been irretrievably 'lost' due to technology failures.

3) Some forms of legislation govern virtually all businesses. The tax authorities may not be too amused to hear that your business won't be submitting any returns for the foreseeable future due to the data having been corrupted and destroyed. In some cases the law also demands that information is kept and made available upon demand for many years after it has been archived. The authorities will not consider 'lost' or 'irretrievable' to mean the same thing as 'archived'.

4) Most companies are, and rightly so, protective of their reputation in their marketplace. Customers and peer group companies may feel uneasy about dealing with a company that has achieved notoriety for major systems failures and difficulty in recovery.

The Options

1) The first step is to think about what is meant by backup and restore, remembering that this may be needed for premises,

equipment, software or data or indeed all four. If you have suffered a major environmental problem such as an office fire, you may need to restart your organization quickly, not only in technology terms, but also from completely different premises.

2) The second thing to analyze is the criticality of your technology infrastructure. For example, you may wish to have everything restored within a maximum of one hour following a major problem. Although that is possible, it may prove unnecessarily expensive. In fact you may need to have a PC running with your customer order system within a few minutes of a problem arising. Areas such as your property management system or General Ledger may be less important for immediate recovery.

FIGURE 5.2   Backing up and disaster recovery are becoming better understood

Having completed these activities, a business should be able to decide what it needs by way of backup and restore. This can then be used to formulate a set of selection criteria for the identification of a backup and recovery solution. Here there are many systems, operations and providers available. These options range from relatively simple and cheap solutions involving e.g. end-of-day automatic backup to CD of master data files that are then stored in an off-site location, right up to a fully duplicated environment deployed on another set of technology elsewhere.

To some extent, the sophistication of your requirements will directly affect the cost of the system you'll put in place. Although the terminology will differ by supplier, some typical systems would include the following (in descending order of complexity and cost).

1) *Full hot-standby mirror site.*

As you work on your systems real-time, duplicated (mirrored) copies of your files are maintained on the disaster standby site at another location. In the event of a catastrophic problem, you can instantly (more or less) switch to an up-to-date mirror version of your system at the other location. These sorts of facilities can include the provision of communications infrastructure and even replacement furniture, PCs and office equipment in an emergency office premises. This is why these are called 'hot-standby' arrangements and predictably they are some of the more expensive options.

2) *Warm standby and partial mirrored sites.*

This is a slight variation on the above where only critical data and systems are stored on the standby site. You may have made alternative, less urgent (and lower cost) arrangements for your other systems to be restored from other sources over the days following a serious problem. This arrangement can also offer slightly deferred start-up times at a target level of say "operational within 3 hours" with the mirror site suppliers as opposed to "operational within 1 hour". All these factors can help reduce the cost of the service.

3) *In-House standby and mirrored systems.*

Environmental disasters that destroy an entire technology infrastructure are, fortunately, very rare. Problems with individual components, systems or databases are much more common. Today's flexible technology offers the possibility to maintain a mirrored 'real time' image of master and critical systems on another file server that sits in the same company. In a problem situation, use of a given system can be switched very quickly to the mirrored system to maintain continuity. This presumes, of course, that the problem has not also affected the mirrored system. If they are well implemented this should be unlikely.

4) *Periodic backups of critical files/systems/data.*

It is possible to automatically take copies of all master databases and critical systems periodically through the day. These copies can be taken offsite over the Internet or to CDs or other storage device in the company. In the event of a crash or problem, the data can be restored to its position at the last time the copies were taken. Although perhaps the cheapest and easiest solution to implement, it is worth noting that this also generates the largest risk (apart from doing nothing!) to a company. If the backups are taken once at the end of a day and a problem corrupts databases at say 4pm, the databases would need to be restored to the position they were in at 6pm the previous day. Potentially a day's work could be irretrievably lost. These solutions can also take some time to restore the backups, test and re-start. A lot of operational time could also possibly be lost.

Backups, storage and recovery systems/solutions remain relatively low cost until one envisages fully mirrored hot-standby etc. Even the costs of putting that in place may pale into insignificance, when considered against the cost of losing your business operation for several days while you rebuild from scratch. For any business, taking the risk of *not* implementing some form of backup and recovery system should be unacceptable.

DOCUMENT MANAGEMENT

Since human beings first started writing on clay tablets and papyrus, managing the storage and retrieval of 'documents' has been of critical importance. The need to do so gave rise to the first libraries in ancient times and the role of the librarian. In ages past, the challenges were considerable but manageable since comparatively few people produced written materials. In more modern times the challenge of maintaining 'order' in the utilization of documents has risen tremendously, as the numbers of documents increased because of advances such as the printing press in the middle ages, the typewriter in the 19th century and the advent of technology / the Internet in the 20th century.

FIGURE 5.3 Document management systems are key when going paperless

All these incredible innovations have, in their time, provided a huge stimulus to publishing, the arts and, of course, business. Yet the resulting proliferation of paper and text has meant that society, and business in particular, has faced major challenges in managing all this information. To state that in the modern business world documents need to be 'managed' may sound blatantly obvious, but in fact this subject is important and deserving of a little in-depth thought.

For a long time, the challenge was seen as exclusively one of how to store the documents so that they can be effectively indexed and retrieved. Today, this is only part of the story because now the key need is the effective dissemination and sharing of knowledge through links into business-wide activities. Businesses can no longer rely on the diligence of an individual to dig thru mountains of versions of documents to find relevant and quickly needed information. Instead they want to see automatic information retrieval and integration into their activities as they progress.

Consider as a start the apparently simple question of 'what is a document?'. In business, the terms 'a document' and 'document management systems' may mean different things to different people. For the purposes of this discussion we'll consider that a document is a consolidation of material (text, figures, images or graphics) to be read. That material may be stored on paper or electronically. The challenges and opportunities for business are no different in either case. It doesn't matter whether the business has created the document or received it, there are certain key considerations in ensuring its most productive use.

- *What purpose does the document serve?*
- *Who owns it? (not necessarily the same thing as authorship)*
- *What activities does it relate to?*
- *Is it static information only or part of a process chain? (e.g. an invoice)*

We will not explore the full range of document analysis techniques in this book. The above are only samples but analyzing documents in this manner clarifies what a business needs to do with a document. How it needs to store and access it will vary.

To give a working example: An invoice from a supplier arrives in the mail in paper format at the same time as a price list from the same supplier. The business receiving these two documents will need to think of them differently. In the first case the invoice needs to be registered as having been received and it then becomes part of an operational process. It needs to be passed to someone to pay it and then filed as 'paid'. The supplier's file record may also need to be updated. Once that is done, except for an audit or annual accounting, the business is unlikely to need to access the invoice again.

The price list however is a permanent reference record that may play a part in day-to-day business operations for an ongoing period. It may need to be accessed continually by the pricing, marketing and finance functions. As a result, not only does it have to be filed but it also needs to be easily accessible and where possible automatically 'flagged' as being available if someone is thinking about preparing (e.g.) a quotation. It will serve little purpose if people do not know it exists.

The same logic applies to documents that the business produces. Whether in paper format or electronic formats, the business needs to know it was produced, with what objective, and to whom it was sent. The ability to effectively store, cross-reference, publicize and retrieve documents is critical. The ability to integrate this with business processes is even more so. The challenges of doing this manually in the modern world can be difficult or even insurmountable – and that is where document management systems come into their own.

A document management system allows a business to convert all its paperwork into electronic format via scanning. Much of the paperwork the business produces may already exist initially in electronic format. Although not quite the paperless office, this is a big step towards it and could largely eliminate paper from the core office areas. Once all paperwork is held electronically, it can be filed and cross-referenced in accordance with the company's needs. This applies not only to general documents but also presentations, spreadsheets, résumés etc.

This information then becomes available to any employee in the business although it is possible to limit areas and secure access so that as appropriate, confidentiality and 'need to see' can be maintained. This immediately reduces the amount of paper consumption because everything can be viewed at the PC screen and precious floor space is saved. Those massive filing cabinets can finally be abolished or at the least, moved into inexpensive offsite premises. It is possible to give the outside world access to certain areas of the system through the Internet. This can be a powerful selling tool as customers often want to be able to 'see' their own files and information in a company and in some cases they may have a legal right to do so.

FIGURE 5.4 Document management can be implemented on or off premises

Although efficient filing and paper savings are important to a business, document management systems can become truly revolutionary for a business when they integrate with business process management and workflow systems. Document management even at its simplest can change the way people work for the better. Consider a comparatively minor example involving a growing business engaged in regular recruitment. In the past, appointments were made in the interviewer's calendar for the candidates. HR would need to remember to send a paper copy of the applicant's résumé and supporting materials to the interviewers. When the files were sent in advance, this led to multiple copies of highly confidential and personal information being distributed around the office in paper form. The risks of loss and contravention of data protection laws (e.g. confidential files and papers left unattended on people's desks) were significantly increased.

Today the candidate's file is scanned once. The interviews are arranged in people's electronic calendars and this entry is set to prompt in advance. When interviewers respond to a prompt, the candidate's file is automatically displayed on the screen for reading. As a result paper is eliminated, risk greatly reduced, and information about the process automatically captured for future optimization activities. Document management is a growing area of business technology and it will play an increasingly critical role for businesses in the future.

BUSINESS OPERATIONS TECHNOLOGIES

BUSINESS INTELLIGENCE (BI)

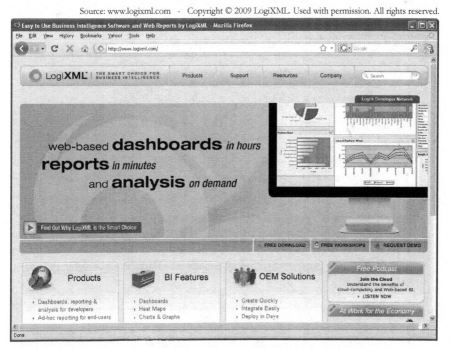

FIGURE 5.5 Newer web-based BI tools are available on the market

For decades businesses have realized that information is key to survival and prosperity. Yet information isn't much use in itself. What is required is the effective exploitation of that information to support informed decision-making. To put it bluntly, information is useless if you do not know you have it, if you do not know where it is, or if you can't get to it.

So, what's the difference between information availability and the ability to exploit that information? For many years business owners sat in meetings trying to answer some basic questions. As a starting point, there's the key question « OK, where do we stand now? » Quickly following on that is the need to understand what the various forms of information available to the business tells owners about opportunities and threats. Finally they need to look to the data to answer questions of "what if?". What if we increase production in the northeast by 15%? What if we reduce costs by 20% on our oldest product?

To answer these questions, traditionally the business owners would sit down and attempt to manually interpret various forms of information coming from various sources in various formats. The accountant may have provided some pertinent accounting related financials from the general ledger while employee offices would have reports indicating labor costs and skills inventories based upon information from the HR system. Marketing may have looked at the sales system and drawn some conclusions about sales successes from the figures. The business collectively then had the challenge of putting all these pieces together and making sense of it.

The information within a business can invariably be held in numerous older (legacy) systems that were implemented to meet specific needs such as accounting, customer billing, sales, HR and so on. They are usually described as 'vertical systems' as they exist to serve the needs of a specific department or business function such as 'sales'. At the end of the day, a business needs to be able to consolidate the information held in these various 'vertical' systems for analysis and interpretation so as to produce an integrated global and horizontal picture. It is even better if this is available real-time.

One approach on the road towards the successful exploitation of this information is to take extracts of these systems and hold the consolidated data in a single repository (or linked repositories) so that it can be accessed and utilized in line with a common set of structures and standards. This business and technical concept is called 'data warehousing'. Once in place, data warehouses can have reporting systems that interpret the consolidated data to produce simplified and multidimensional views of the business. Today this approach has to some extent been superseded by the recognition that the effort and cost involved in creating huge data warehouses and specific reports may prove prohibitive. There is now more emphasis on extracting and utilizing information, as it exists in the organization's departmental systems to produce simplified business metrics.

FIGURE 5.6 Flexibility and ease of use are required in today's BI systems

Whether the base information resides in the departmental systems or a central data warehouse, manual consolidation and interpretation would be a near impossible task due to the volumes and complexities involved without this technology. Such software is usually called Business Intelligence or sometimes Decision Support System. Its basic function is to bring together and interpret the various sources of information available to the business. This information may have its origin in any internal system from sales to accounting through to HR.

It may also utilize information fed into the business from external sources such as stock prices or news feeds.

The job of a Business Intelligence system is to interpret the relationships and linkages between key elements of the stored data and to present these to the business based on defined rules, in a form that is easy to understand. For example, if the staff turnover rate this quarter is higher than predicted, BI technology may show this as one reason that the forecast for production figures was significantly higher than actual. New staff takes time to train and are unlikely to be as productive immediately as more experienced staff.

As such, the function of a Business Intelligence System can be seen as one of 'consolidation' 'Integration' 'interpretation' and 'representation' of the underlying data. The representation of the information after consolidation is key. In today's hectic business world, managers and business owners need to see 'at a glance' what's happening. This need has led to the development of new approaches to the presentation of business information. No longer are there vast reports containing millions of figures. In Business Intelligence systems, there is now much emphasis on the presentation of facts, trends and options in highly consolidated graphical form. There are many forms of these but two of the most well known are 'Scorecards' and 'Dashboards'.

In a successful Business Intelligence System, the business owners and decision makers will be able to look at scorecards that define their departmental or business performance, measured by their own defined targets and, if relevant, the performance of their competitors. The scorecard is usually a simplified graphical representation of e.g. performance by department against target. The second form of presentation is the dashboard. These formats closely resemble the dashboard instrumentation of a modern car. They are the representation of instruments that show aspects of the way the business is performing. These may include profit, sales, staff turnover and so on. These can be monitored on a daily basis as the indicators of the business's health can be seen moving as they are constantly updated. This allows immediate corrective or opportunistic action to be taken as these indicators (sometimes called KPIs for Key

Performance Indicators) shift.

The speedometer in a car may start to fall as the car climbs a hill. The reaction to that may be to apply more gas. The same principle would apply to a business performance dashboard. Seeing that production levels are dropping at the same time that HR sickness stats are rising would highlight to the business that perhaps extra temporary staff is needed quickly to maintain production levels.

Key to the successful implementation and exploitation of any Business Intelligence System is its ability to access the base information it needs and to interpret and consolidate this in line with an agreed set of business rules. For any business, large or small, this may demand as much change of culture in the organization as it does technical change. If the leaders think and operate vertically as fiefdoms and silos then trying to force a Business Intelligence System horizontally across the business will fail.

Business Intelligence Systems are revolutionizing business practice, but they are having the maximum impact in those companies that have set themselves up in cooperative and non-vertical organizational structures in readiness for the new 21st century world. Midsize and small businesses can certainly benefit from BI technology, but only when the time is right. When the business is optimal operationally, BI is a good logical step to gaining deeper insights into the business for growth and evolution. There are many business intelligence systems on the market including products from companies such as Cognos, LogiXML and Actuate.

ENTERPRISE RESOURCE PLANNING/ INTEGRATED BUSINESS MANAGEMENT

Even in the smallest of businesses, the relationships between various aspects of the business are many and varied. Trying to keep them all in mind and understanding all the inter-dependencies can be a mind-boggling task for a small business. For midsize and large businesses it can become virtually impossible. In addition, trying to understand the effect of change in one area upon another can be daunting. Consider for a moment the company that receives a phone call from a customer asking if a large order can be filled next week.

115

This can be a trickier question that it appears at face value. Before deciding whether to answer 'yes' or 'no', the person concerned has to know:

- *What does our current order list look like and what will have to 'give' to fit this order in?*
- *Do we have the staff available or are key employees on vacation next week?*
- *Are any of the production machines "down" for service/repair in the immediate future?*
- *Will we need additional raw materials to meet the order?*
- *Do we have sufficient time to order the materials and sufficient cash-in-hand to pay for them?*
- *Can our suppliers deliver on time?*
- *Is this customer's credit history good or do we need to ask for cleared payment in advance?*

It would be easy to continue this list for some time! Traditionally many businesses would make the decision to accept the order above, and *then* go after the answers to those questions. Alternatively, other companies have invested in production planning and control systems that helped, but as they frequently did not link to personnel and finance systems, they only provided a partial picture of what was or was not possible.

Although this may have been workable for smaller businesses, many will privately admit that, more than once, they've made bad decisions and lost customers simply because they did not have all the up to date information. Promises may have been made to do something 'next week' only to subsequently discover that it was not possible. Internally, someone had forgotten to tell someone else about a missing batch of parts or that information on the financial report was not yet updated to reflect the latest orders processed. Complaints about this usually resulted in lengthy explanations that system A was not yet up-o-date and had to be 2 or 3 days behind system B because system B needed information from system C that was manually produced, etc!

FIGURE 5.7 ERP systems deliver the functional modules needed to run a business

Several years ago most large companies decided that enough was enough and that a better system was needed. Many such companies started to install ERP (Enterprise Resource Planning) systems to address the lack of integrated business systems. These ERP systems basically delivered all the required modules to run a business fully integrated, served by a master reference repository, with transactions flowing real-time across business functions. The way the company worked would be centrally controlled; it would be prioritized, scheduled and governed by a set of uniform and integrated business processes. No longer would questions such as *"can we…"* or *"where is the blockage/opportunity…."* be dependent for an answer upon someone's gut instinct or information that's not up-to-date.

In the beginning, these systems were large, complicated and invariably very expensive, coming from a few major software suppliers. They tended to be seen as 'mega-corporation' systems with multi-million dollar price tags, and multi-year implementation timelines. That's all history now. The suppliers of such systems have long since recognized that the world also comprises medium and smaller companies running smaller PC and server-based systems. Smaller businesses are as much in need of integrated business management as the larger ones. To reflect this, there are now a number of 'one system' solutions for smaller businesses comprising all the core business function modules that a business needs. They're affordable though still somewhat pricey for some small businesses. Quickbooks Enterprise, SAP One and SAGE MAS90 are a few of the packages that have been around for some time now.

What do they do? It is perhaps easiest to answer this question with an example. Let's assume that you've placed an order for a new file server with your technology supplier. The integrated system will allow you to generate the purchase order through the purchasing module. It can send the PO electronically to the supplier. It can also post an accrual entry (i.e. "there's a bill due in") notification to the General Ledger module and a 'Due In' notification to the Fixed Assets module. Once the PC is delivered and noted as 'received' by your receiving department, the Fixed Assets module will automatically note it as 'on the premises' and could start posting capital asset depreciation to the General Ledger module. This will automatically update the Accounts Payable module to say that the supplier's invoice can be paid when received.

In all of this, the processes would be largely automated. No paper would be passed around and more importantly, there would be no custom interfaces between business modules or re-typing of information. Nobody has to remember to update the Fixed Assets system because it is a module of the Integrated Business Management system which is updated automatically. Similar benefits can be obtained with almost any core business process. For example, the stock control system can automatically recognize when levels have fallen to a specified re-order point and issue the order automatically. At the same time it can update the General Ledger and Accounts Payable modules as they're all part of the same system.

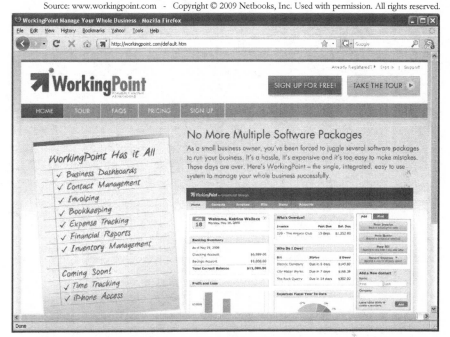

FIGURE 5.8 Integrated business systems are well adapted for smaller business

The savings for businesses can be big. Not only is manual intervention reduced and things speeded up, but errors are also significantly reduced. Now when a customer asks "can you do this next week?" anyone in the business can see, at a glance, the stock position, the production capacity, staff availability and details of the customer's financial status. Information is fully up-to-date and integrated to give a single composite view.

Integrated business management has proven its value and has moved into the domain of the midsize and small business. It is revolutionizing the way many of them do business and should be an objective for businesses of all sizes. Major ERP / Integrated Business Management systems sit at the core of most larger companies, from banks to manufacturing operations, and those that do not use them are in the process of getting there.

BUSINESS PROCESS MANAGEMENT

One of the most commonly shared customer experiences most of us have had is to find oneself thinking *"... am I having to do it this way for their benefit or mine?"* Now it may be that you've been unlucky and have just encountered an employee who is incompetent or who's having a bad day. In many cases though, when as customers we find ourselves receiving poor service from a company, this is likely to be due to the business's poorly implemented business processes rather than inept employees.

Many business structures have been set up on an essentially hierarchical basis. In other words, if you sketched their organizational structure you'd end up with something more or less resembling a pyramid with one person or a few people at the top. It's therefore not surprising that many larger businesses were run, and continue to be run, on the same basis. At the top, sits the board or owners and reporting to them is the President or the CEO. Reporting to the president/CEO are various departmental or function heads, each of whom is in charge of their particular part of the business. In turn each head of a department has turned their department into his/her own pyramid with him/her at the top.

In reality, many large companies have evolved what are termed 'vertical' operations. The head of Finance had his/her own hierarchical structure and naturally built his own internal processes to run it accordingly. The same is true for HR, Sales, Marketing, Manufacturing and so on. While optimizing processes within a vertical organization may work to optimize that department's process, maintaining a deep and ongoing understanding of those defined processes is a continuous challenge. Additionally, developing, maintaining and owning business processes that run across the traditional functional areas was an even greater challenge.

Managing the operation of a business with many different departments, to ensure that the various departments interact even half-efficiently is complex, time-consuming and expensive. Many businesses found they were employing far more staff in internal co-ordination and supervision to make the company work, than in making and selling their products. This was not and is not, sustainable in a competitive world.

The move to a customer-centric, more competitive business environment means that customers are increasingly demanding exemplary service. They want things done 'their way' rather than in a manner dictated by the business's rigid processes. No longer are they prepared (e.g.) to provide the same information twice just because the supplier's ordering and delivery departments sit in two different areas using disconnected processes. The customer is more and more prepared to walk away and find a business that does it 'his/her way'.

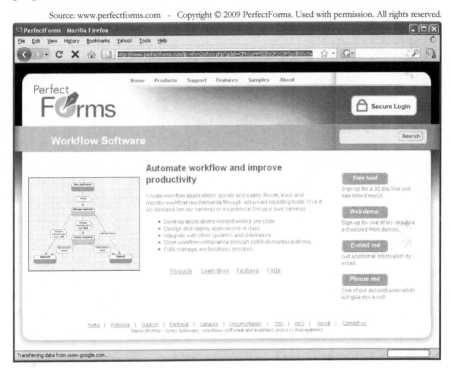

FIGURE 5.9 Current BPM tools address all levels of business process complexity

Larger companies are increasingly looking at Business Process Management (BPM) as a way of changing the way they think about their business activities and how they operate. BPM forces a business to ask questions about the way it conducts its operations or manages itself. It demands thinking in terms of business operations and technology processes and the interconnections between them. What

BPM essentially looks at is re-focusing of attention and investment in the business onto what is needed to deliver a successful business process irrespective of hierarchies and organizational structures.

As an example, many large businesses would consider that the act of taking a customer order and billing are different. One goes into the order-processing department and from there perhaps to the shipping department. Eventually the accounts department will send the invoice out. Each of these departments has their own process. There is an order process, a shipping process and an invoicing process. Each department built their process to meet the best standards of order processing, shipping and billing. Each department will have its head that reports up the vertical line, etc.

The customer, however, does not see it this way. To the customer, there is one process: placing their order, getting the product, and getting billed the right amount quickly. If there is a problem –they're not interested in demarcation disputes between the three departments or spending all their time being transferred between the three departments to find what's gone wrong and where. BPM would argue that the selling company here should not only be thinking about optimizing department processes, but also constructing one 'customer order' process that integrates all three processes into one horizontal process.

Historically, technology systems were implemented to support existing hierarchical structures. There was therefore an order processing system, a shipping system and a billing system. Where they needed to share information, interfaces were built between them. Under BPM, technology systems are implanted to support integrated process management rather than a department's structure. In our hypothetical case, this means that instead of three individual systems that need to interface, there is now one logical 'customer servicing' system.

BPM can address the issues of defining and implementing a horizontal process across the business that's already well supported by appropriately aligned technology. The end-to-end horizontal process must be managed by an end-to-end management system. This is what BPM does for you, in addition to fully documenting and maintaining the processes that would otherwise sit in people's heads or on some obscure shelf somewhere. These are modern technology systems that can define the processes and present information and prompts to key staff so that the new process can be seen and managed as an entity rather than a series of disjointed departmental activities.

Business Process Management is a complex subject which is still evolving in big business but is also readily available for smaller businesses. It calls for change in business culture, technology systems and the way a business sees and manages itself. It cannot be implemented by simply purchasing a piece of software or changing departmental descriptions, job titles or demarcations.

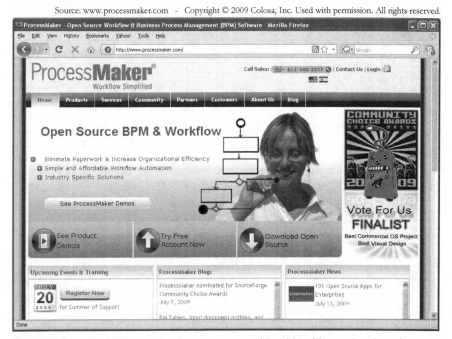

FIGURE 5.10 The BPM market has grown considerably with good options for tools

It demands fundamental re-thinking about the way the business functions, to what objectives, and how it will manage itself en-route to those objectives.

A midsize and small business can gain some great learning from bigger brother/sister. Either start off by implementing integrated

123

business systems at the earliest time possible, or be prepared to deal with the vertical walls created when it has grown up. While BPM technology may not be highly leverage-able now for small businesses, the modelling and implementation of processes and the use of workflow tools can be a business saver further down the road.

WORKFORCE MANAGEMENT

People can be a company's greatest asset but paradoxically, also one of its greatest liabilities. It's not easy deploying staff in a way that best utilizes their skills and capabilities yet keeps them fully occupied, motivated and appropriately rewarded (financially and psychologically) at the same time. In many businesses, people are the greatest single cost component of the operation. If they are not managed effectively, it is a huge waste of the business's resources and a lost opportunity. The challenges of getting the best from employees are not new. Companies have always struggled in this area.

FIGURE 5.11 HR tools are well developed and should be leveraged by businesses

It is important to differentiate at the start between three types of workforce management. The first may be described as the mechanistic and relatively 'fixed' components of workforce management and administration. Those areas such as payroll, personnel records, timecards and pensions, have all long since been automated and (hopefully!) no longer give companies great cause for concern. These were among the very first business areas to become automated as far back as the 1950s. There are many relatively stable systems available today that will handle these functions very well and we address some of them in this book. In a sense, they are the easier areas to get right.

The second category is the effective allocation of employees to address business issues and opportunities. This is a more dynamic area where complexities can easily arise. To ensure that a workforce is optimally utilized means that the potential, strengths and weaknesses of the workforce must be readily known. This includes understanding:

Who is currently doing what?
Who possesses what skills?
Who is highly productive and who is less so?
Who is joining and when?
Who needs what (e.g. training) and when?
Who is peaking out?
Who is emerging as talent?

This is not a comprehensive list but it illustrates the sort of issues that a business needs to have on demand to effectively draw on the best within its ranks. This is more important for large businesses that have employees 10 to 15 levels deep, but it is also of importance for the growing small business. It is then necessary to merge the above knowledge of the potential with work demand and strategic priorities and make 'best utilization' and work assignment decisions accordingly. As a requirement, this is nothing new. Few managers will admit that they do not really know their workforce, what they are doing or that they are incapable of allocating them where required. In the case of a very small company with perhaps only 2-3 staff, keeping the above information in a single spreadsheet or in one's head may work for a while. However, for an operation that's larger or growing, that will prove difficult or, at best, highly ineffective.

People are not a static resource. They may have skills that may be in need of refreshing. In other cases they may be short of skills and need to be trained. Some people are ambitious and expect career development and advancement while others become unhappy at being asked to take on additional responsibility. These variables need to be understood and their relevance to work assignments taken into account. If they are not, staff disaffection will increase, productivity and quality will fall, and rising staff turnover will shortly follow both. Staff resignation and recruitment is a big expense that can be highly disruptive to normal business and customer service.

Source: www.wfmsg.com - © 2009 The Workforce Management Software Group, Inc. Used with permission.

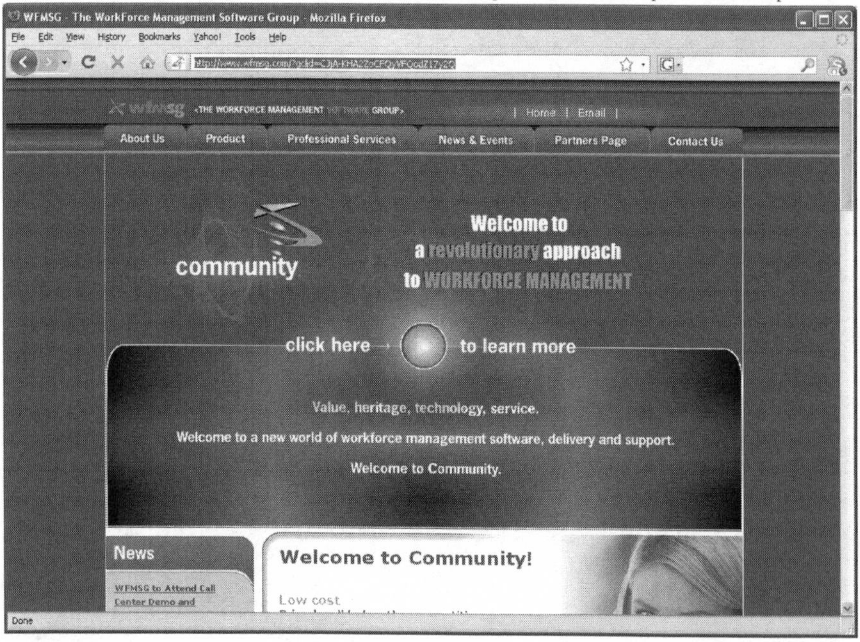

FIGURE 5.12 Some companies are looking at ways to innovate the HR process

There are many symptoms that indicate when a workforce is not being effectively managed. Some of these symptoms are 'internal' and others 'external'. Internal issues are usually visible only to the staff and company concerned. They may include:

- Employees needing to remind bosses that a performance review or pay increase is overdue.
- Managers desperately looking for an individual only to be told that they're on vacation.
- People sitting around for periods with little or nothing to do while others are hopelessly overloaded.
- Delays in activities, quality issues and poor productivity because staff allocated to a task do not possess all the pre-requisite skills.
- People double-booked to two different activities at the same time.
- Increased staff disaffection and turnover.
- Executives who are unable to see a composite picture of workforce utilization or capacity.

Externally, these problems can also be visible to customers. Many have experienced going into a shop or bank and seeing a long queue at one desk, while at others, staff seem to have little to do other than stare into space. Customers have been told their work is going to be delayed because nobody knew the person allocated was going on vacation. Staff admitting to customers they're not sure what they're doing because they haven't been trained. None of these situations creates a positive impression and frequently results in the customer going elsewhere.

There is now a new generation of software products that can help business to get a handle on all of these issues. Workforce management software comprises a number of modules. The terminology may change between suppliers, but these essentially help a business manage areas such as:

Workforce Development / Skills Inventory

These functions allow training needs, employee potential and performance reviews to be automatically taken into account in work plans. Events can be diarized and reminders generated. It can also link

127

to supporting HR and personnel systems.

Staff Work Scheduling

These modules relate the company's needs for staff (e.g. order book or work planning systems) to the availability of staff. This would automatically take into account vacations, skill levels and other deployments etc. Full automatic scheduling of work down to individual level can be achieved. This can automatically reflect changes in real time as they happen.

Contracts

These functions provide the capability to manage employees that are engaged on client activities in or out-of-office. The client's specific needs and requirements are automatically factored in and employees are scheduled against that in line with needs.

Performance Analysis & Summary

Performance 'on the job' can be tracked and measured. This information can be summarized for management information via the use of 'dashboard' type information summaries that offer the capability to support drilling-down into base detail for individual work assignments or employee.

Employee Self-Service

Staff can inspect and update their own personal details and skills inventories etc. This improves staff satisfaction and the accuracy of information. Free access of the individual to their personal data and its accurate maintenance may be a legal requirement in some jurisdictions. The effective utilization of resource through Workforce Management Systems can reduce overheads, improve productivity, create higher customer satisfaction levels, and make for a happier workplace. It is something worth considering!

OFFICE SUITE

Every business needs to create documents in its operations. There is also a constant need to manage financial information, performing ad-hoc calculations and reports. The business needs to create professional materials to present new ideas, concepts, and products to potential customers and investors. An all-in-one office suite can provide these capabilities. An office suite, sometimes called a productivity suite, includes programs that can be used for word processing, creating spreadsheets as well as digital presentations. Other common features are email and note-taking functions. These technology capabilities are indispensible business tools.

FIGURE 5.13 Office suite software are indispensible business productivity tools

Word processing (WP) has come a long way since its humble origins as a slightly clever way of manipulating text. This type of software has been around since the 1960s. Originally running on specialized computers and systems, during the 1980s, word processing software moved into the domain of the 'normal' desktop PC or server.

129

Now it is increasingly moving onto mobile computing devices. Today's WP software is very powerful. Most packages of this type can produce output in a vast array of font types, styles and colors. We now take for granted its ability to spell and syntax check as we type – and this in just about any language we choose. It's also possible to incorporate tables, images and graphics into the final product. Many companies that previously had to send out their text and materials for professional typesetting and printing (e.g. manuals), now produce very high quality results internally. Good progress has been made also with integrating voice-recognition systems into WP. It's perhaps 'not quite there yet'; but its coming!

The ability to tabulate and calculate across numbers is now considered basic. Spreadsheets have been around on small computers for a long time and they are now very powerful and sophisticated. It's possible to define very complicated formulas and complex reports. The figures can be instantly converted to graphs. There is also the ability to link spreadsheets so that they can be used as data collection and consolidation system for activities such as expenses reporting. Some businesses have managed to build fairly sophisticated accounting and other financial systems using spreadsheets. However this is *not* recommended. The long-term requirements to manage such systems can become extremely expensive and unwieldy. There are standalone financial packages, as well as modules within integrated business management systems, available to support such needs.

Standing before an audience and giving a presentation, whether in person or by remote is not easy. Having good graphics, slides and other materials, can augment a presentation so that it communicates much more effectively, while being much less intimidating for the presenter. Modern presentation software is extremely easy to use and very flexible. It offers the ability to integrate graphics, text, images and even video. The output can be printed onto the traditional slides as well as delivered as electronic presentation packs over a videoconference or other form of computer conferencing system.

Keeping track of your calendar and scheduled events including all phone numbers, email addresses and inter-dependencies can be a complex activity. Having calendar and personal management software can greatly reduce the stresses and mishaps in this area. These systems can also interface with mobile computing systems such as smart phones. If you're out talking with a client, you can access your full calendar systems 'back at base' and make any changes in real-time.

There are many forms of software of the 'office suite' variety offered for free on the Internet and but one must exercise extra caution before downloading. Remember that if you're using a proprietary product such as a spreadsheet and need to send a file from it to another location, the person at the other end will need to be able to open it and use it. Compatibility may be an issue with some very specialized office tools products downloaded free from the Internet.

FIGURE 5.14 OpenOffice, with its free office suite, attempts to change the game

Many are sold individually and some as software 'bundles'. Perhaps the best known of these is the Microsoft Office Suite (usually just known as MS Office or Office). Many of the above facilities plus several others can be purchased as the typical MS Office bundle. The individual components of a bundled package of office products are unlikely to be 'state of the art' in terms of their functions and facilities, but they should offer reliability and the ability to work together without hassle. An alternative is to look for free software of the above types through the Internet. Of these the best known is perhaps the Open Office suite of programs that offers free versions of sophisticated word processing packages, spreadsheets and presentation software. Although they may lack some exotic components of some of the purchasable packages, they are likely to be perfectly adequate for many small business operations. The fact that they are free is a major attraction, however, it is best to test drive before making a decision.

BUSINESS FINANCE TECHNOLOGIES

PAYROLL SYSTEMS

Some technologies like e-commerce, websites, remote applications, automatic transaction systems and such, all have a glamorous ring to them. By contrast, nothing is likely to generate yawns faster than the subject of a 'payroll system'. If you're already finding that you're stifling a yawn at the thought of reading about payroll software – remember one thing. Payroll is without exception the most used and, in terms of output, the best-checked system in any company large or small.

It doesn't matter what line of business you're in, you and all employees want to see that paycheck each month. The staff in shipping may only look at the shipping system and have no interest in the accounts systems. The accounts people probably couldn't care less about the shipping system, and the customer order processing people may not give two hoots what the external supplier management system is doing. You can be 101% sure that each month everybody, from the CEO downwards, will care very much indeed about what the Payroll system is up to.

If the paychecks aren't produced on time, a business's operations can stop dead. If they're produced on time but wrong, the questioning and resolution activities can be very high and a lot of productive time is going to be lost. If an employee is expecting 1000 dollars on their paycheck but instead finds only 850, it is a fair bet that they're unlikely to give their undivided attention to their job until it's resolved. Cue the irate phone calls and in the more extreme cases, the thumping on the payroll office's door!

FIGURE 5.15 Payroll systems have moved online and most are pretty mature

Payroll is often a far more complicated operation than many people will acknowledge. In a very small business, perhaps traditionally the owner would manually compute what people were due and pay them directly by check or even cash. This, though, starts to become difficult when there are more than a few employees or if the amounts to be paid are not fixed by hours. Variable time working, shifts, allowances, salary advances, timesheets, absence records and deductions - they all start to generate a vast administrative overhead. The knowledge and skills required for successful payroll operation are not trivial. In many companies, the 'payroll administrator' was one of the most important people in the company and often more widely feared than the CEO or business owner. Their operation of the payroll each week or month was often perceived by others in the company to be something of a 'dark-art'.

Today however, most large businesses have moved to full automation of this area and many companies have had computerized payroll systems in place for years. Those companies that have not adopted an automated system and are considering doing so usually have a number of specific objectives, including:

- *To reduce the amount of manual work required*
- *To reduce errors*
- *To reduce or eliminate disputes and requests for clarifications*
- *To improve employee service and satisfaction*
- *To empower employees via self-service systems and operations*
- *To improve compliance with laws and regulations*
- *To eliminate the risk of being dependent upon a single expert (or two)*
- *To reduce the cost of operation or 'cost-to-serve' as it may be called*
- *To better understand where their payroll spend is going and on what*

In the marketplace today, there are many payroll systems for sale. They range in price from some that are offered virtually free, to others that offer function-rich capabilities at a cost of tens of thousands of dollars. It is beyond the scope of this article to describe any one of them in detail, but let's look at some of their functionalities in terms of the above objectives.

There is no logical reason why pieces of paper must be sent by employees to the payroll office detailing things such as expenses claims, hours worked, and so on. This information can be captured automatically from timesheet systems at a PC or via employee input. This is then held in the system for validation by the payroll office and 'due process'. Equally, there is no need for payroll staff to require vast numbers of desktop calculators to work things out. The various rate rules and allowances can all be calculated automatically. Errors are reduced because information is validated and verified at the point where it is captured, rather than several days later when the paycheck is produced or someone in payroll notices it.

FIGURE 5.16 Online payroll services are real and reliable options for businesses

Many modern payroll systems offer facilities for employees to take a greater degree of personal responsibility for the accuracy of their data. Through the system, employees can be given access to their own timesheet information, absence records and the calculations used to arrive at their net pay. They can review this in advance and if there are errors, these can be corrected in conjunction with payroll operations staff. This will help to reduce disputes and unnecessary questions later. Through these systems, employees can also maintain their own records in some areas – a good example would be changes of address or next-of-kin information. In some jurisdictions, there may be a legal and accounting requirement to produce reports and statistics relating to employees and payments, etc. These reports can be produced automatically. Payroll systems are designed to operate in accordance with specified rules and calculations. No longer do these sit in someone's head, meaning that the business is not seriously exposed each year during his/her annual vacation or if they're off sick. The reduction in manual labor to produce the payroll should also result in some good cost savings.

Most modern payroll systems can produce easy-to-understand reports and graphs showing exactly where a business is spending its money and on what. Full diagrams can be produced showing analytics that cover every aspect of the operation, including who is getting paid by fixed or variable hours, allowances, expenses claims, absence analyses and so on. This is an invaluable tool for management.

While on the subject of payroll, it is important to conclude with a mention of the above. It is possible to 'outsource' the entire operation of your payroll to an external bureau. It will keep and maintain all the software and hardware and handle all employee calls and questions. All you have to do is feed them, each week or month, the necessary raw information (e.g. timesheets) to produce your reports and paychecks. It can mean a significant reduction in the cost of your payroll department, as the external company is now, to a large extent, your payroll department. There are pros and cons to these types of service that mean it may not be the best option for all companies. But if you're having a radical re-think about the way you do things, then a look at this option may be worthwhile. Be prepared to ask for professional help before making a decision on this.

ACCOUNTING SYSTEMS

Companies that don't pay too much attention to accounting (and there are a surprising number) tend not to stay in business for very long! Some businesses see accounting as a chore and a largely administrative function. That's regrettable because good accounting supported by a good account system is almost as important to the success of a company as the dreaming up of that new product or the sales force.

Let's think of accounting as serving three basic functions. The first of these is regulatory. Depending upon legal jurisdictions and the type of business concerned, accounting needs to communicate various things to the outside world about how a business is doing. Getting this wrong or deciding that you cannot be bothered about it can quickly lead to the demise of the business. What's actually required here will vary but it may include the need to report profit and loss, a balance sheet, employee statistics, etc. The second function of accounting systems is to administer certain aspects of the 'money side' of an organization. Examples of this include Accounts Payable or Accounts Receivables – ensuring that people's invoices are paid punctually and that money due is coming in when it should and is deposited where it should be. The third function of accounting is to provide the company with metrics relating to the performance of their business. In a sense, this is often of the most important parts of accounting systems, in terms of longer term strategy for a business.

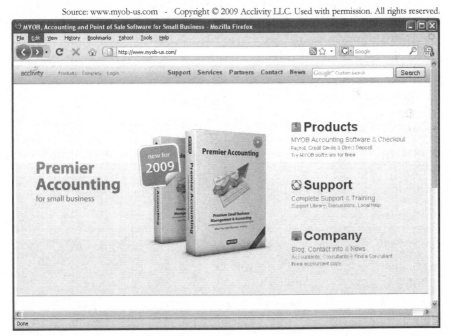

FIGURE 5.17 Accounting software for small business are very robust and stable

This is the financial dashboard that shows the health of the business, where it is underperforming, where it's going well and where opportunities may exist in future. It also provides the company with a powerful reality check in terms of providing a view of what is achievable financially speaking and what may be an equally good idea, but one that cannot be funded as things stand.

In this context, accounting systems play a crucial role as part of a Management Information System. It is really for the third reason that modern accounting systems and accountants (or CFO in many larger businesses) have changed so much in the past few years. The days when accounting systems and accountants were seen only as "keeping the books" are long gone. The accounting system is a dynamic developer of a business and accountants are key partners in making things happen for the business as a whole. Accounting systems have evolved to meet these challenges. Of course the basic functions of regulatory reporting and administrative capabilities remain important. Bills have to be paid, cash flow needs to be monitored and clients have to be persuaded to pay their bills. However, today many accounting systems are now selected for their added ability to contribute to the third dimension above – i.e. how can they help manage and develop the business going forward?

There are large numbers of very reasonably priced accounting systems to choose from. Many come with support built-in for basic accounting functions such as Payables, Receivables, Cash Flow Management, Profit & Loss Calculations, Taxation Management, Balance Sheet production and statutory reporting for various governmental institutions.

Of course, all these functions can only be as accurate (and therefore successful) as the data that is put into them. This can at times be a problem because there may not be much point to having a sophisticated core accounting system if many of the organization's other systems continue to be paper or spreadsheet based. The re-keying effort could be significant and the error percentages high, as a result.

If an integrated business management system is not in place, linking the accounting package automatically to 'feeder' systems such as the order processing, purchasing and payroll systems may be a very good idea to improve accuracy and timeliness. A key benefit of accounting systems comes with their ability to interpret the data they're receiving and thereby deliver key financial reporting and financial management information to the business on a daily, weekly or monthly basis. As an example, before making a large 'yes/no' spending decision, the people leading a business may want to know what their basic money position is and that they're going to stay within bank agreed limits etc. This may sound easy, but to know this one needs to understand:

- *How much cash is in the bank?*
- *How much is known to be en-route?*
- *When is the en-route cash likely to arrive?*
- *What existing commitments are in place that also need to be paid for soon (accruals)?*

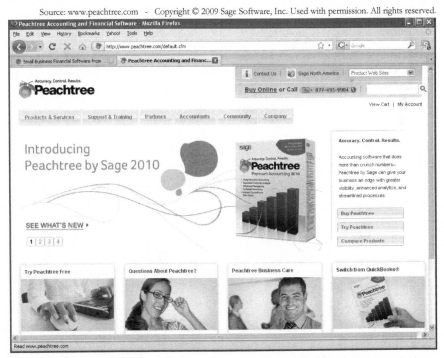

FIGURE 5.18 Peachtree is one of several top tools for small business accounting

The traditional way to achieve this was to ask the accounting department for a report and this would arrive containing lots of figures for interpretation. Today the same information can be available daily on the PC 'at a glance' in a graphical dashboard format. The need for this sort of information to support decision-making can be as sophisticated as the business needs. It is possible to see on a graph the total company expenditure during a period, so as to give a view of where the organization is spending its money at a point in time. Many of these packages now also come with powerful trend analysis tools. They can show where spend and income has been, where it currently is, and what that means for the period or periods ahead. So if you're wondering what increasing spending in one area may mean for profits, the software will be able to give some projections for this based upon what it knows about the past.

SUMMARY

Hopefully this chapter has shown you two things. The first is that there is no single technology that you can implement for your business that will make it the last word in efficiency. The second thing is that no matter what your situation is, there is a technology solution that *will* help your business become more efficient and cost effective, for a price that is right for the solution. However, targeting an integrated business management solution for your business is absolutely the way to go, and is a big step in an even better optimized future. Technology consultants that specialize in using technology to help businesses become more efficient are plentiful. A small investment by you in some guidance *before* buying new technology will help to ensure that your new technology really will make your business more efficient – as it should.

CHAPTER 6

NEW BUSINESS MEDIUM TECHNOLOGIES

Almost everyone has purchased something on-line at least once. For many people, it is the way they purchase almost all the things they buy. The advantages to offering products and services on-line are numerous, especially for a smaller business. Low transaction costs, greater number of purchases, a whole new set of customers – going on-line can mean exponential growth for your business.

All of the new mediums through which you can interact with customers, provide goods and services to customers, and deal with suppliers starts with creating an on-line presence for your business. There are challenges. For small business, it can be difficult to get customers to come to your website, and even more difficult to attract returning visitors. And competition in the e-commerce world is growing more intense every year as it becomes easier to set up shop. But the potential is enormous! Let's take a closer look at just what it means to do business on-line.

WHAT IS E-COMMERCE?

At its most basic level, e-commerce (an abbreviation for "electronic commerce") is simply about doing business with your customers over the internet – and ideally that should be how simple your customers find the process. But there is a lot more going on that the business owner needs to understand and take care of on their end. E-commerce is part of an overall e-business strategy. The two terms tend to be used interchangeably – but generally e-business focuses on how electronic methods of business are employed, while e-commerce refers to the business processes themselves. For this book, we are going to simplify and just discuss the whole subject as e-commerce.

Business-to-consumer (B2C) e-commerce refers to transactions between a business like yours and customers who are individual consumers. Business-to-business (B2B) e-commerce refers to transactions between businesses. The terms are mentioned here because you will hear them in business and marketing magazines. But the distinction is somewhat artificial. The e-commerce tools you need for both types of commerce are the same. Again, we are going to simplify by discussing selling goods and services on-line, regardless of who the customer is. No matter what your e-commerce setup is, whether you are selling goods or services, selling through your own website or someone else's, you need to think about the following:

- How you interact with your customers through the website including how the orders are dealt with (back office transactions)
- Payment options
- Security for your e-commerce site

Let's look at details on how e-commerce can apply to your small business.

E-COMMERCE TECHNOLOGIES FOR YOUR WEBSITE

To really exploit the potential of the Internet as a sales and operations channel, it is necessary to ensure your internet presence is

142

more sophisticated than a mere content based site and that you move to a transaction based web site. Let's discuss some of the capabilities that your business will need to implement an e-commerce solution through your website.

UPDATING INVENTORY FROM BACK END APPLICATIONS

The logical first step to being able to sell your products or services on-line is showing what you have to sell. The key to showing what you have to sell is tying your inventory of goods to your website through a back office database software package. In this way, your customers will be able to see what you have to offer, and the availability of the products will always be up to date. The technology you will need to do this will depend on the type of database you are using to store your inventory. The nice thing here is that this is such a common requirement that all the major databases are now designed to export information so that it can be used with a webpage.

Usually it works like this: a customer goes to your webpage that shows all widgets made by manufacturer XYZ. Your webpage uses a Java or Javascript program to *query* the inventory database, asking it for all widgets made by XYZ. The database retrieves the information and supplies it to the program, which then *makes the webpage in real time* to send to the potential customer. With this technology, your web pages are built by the program as they are needed by your customer. In effect, you have a template for your pages that is then filled in by your inventory database. Of course, there is a bit of work to get things running smoothly, and the odds are you need some professional help to actually implement the solution.

Of course, if you are selling services that are relatively static and do not really change over time, your job is even easier. You won't need to worry about this step at all. In this case, building a static web page that describes each service will be more than adequate.

SHOPPING CARTS

With your inventory database now tied to your webpage, you now need a way for the customer to place an order. The technology that provides this feature is commonly known as a "shopping cart". The shopping cart is a program running along with your website that keeps track of what a customer selects to buy. The idea comes from a customer being able to "look into their shopping cart" at the store to see what they are going to purchase. This is the simple part of the technology. The second half of the shopping cart is for the customer to "check out" their items, i.e. telling the website that they are done shopping and now want to pay.

At this stage, the shopping cart will walk the customer through confirming the items to be ordered, getting the customer to provide payment and billing details, and finally confirming that the entire order has been completed. For the user, the checkout should be just that simple. However, the shopping cart is doing a lot more work in the background. First off, it needs to be notifying accounts that a payment has just been received. It then has to tell the inventory database to update its available quantity for the items purchased.

Generally, if you are hiring outside help to set up your e-commerce solution, the shopping cart, integration with the inventory database, and handling e-payments are the core components that the company will deliver to you.

SEARCH FUNCTIONS

Have you ever tried to shop at an on-line store, only to have a terrible time finding the items you want to buy? The layout of the website is important for making it easy for customers to find what they are looking for. A potential customer often knows exactly what they are looking for and all they want to look at is that one item. Because of this, a well made search function for your e-commerce site is essential. A very common approach is to use Google to supply search capabilities for your site. This can usually be done for a very modest price and is normally quite effective. However, if you are going to have a lot of items in your database that are normally searched in specific ways, it may be worth having the expert who is helping you set up your e-commerce solution also create a search function for the site. Just make sure that no matter how you set up your search function, your customers can find what they are looking for!

USING A 3ʳᴰ PARTY MARKETPLACE

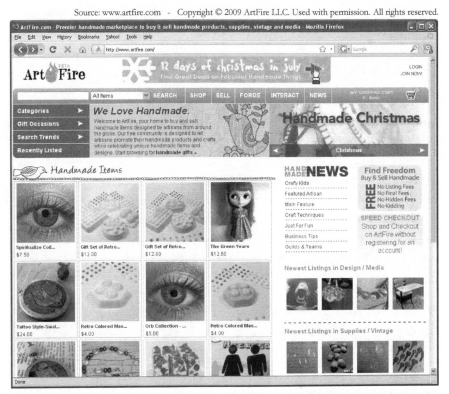

FIGURE 5.6 These sites are alternatives to setting up and marketing your own site

A small business just starting out may not have the finances to develop its own e-commerce solution from scratch. But don't despair! There is still a way for you to enjoy the benefits and sales of e-commerce while you are building your business. Instead of building your own website, you can sell your goods and services through a third party marketplace. A marketplace is similar to a bazaar – you pay for your space in the store, either through a commission on each sale or a flat fee per month. In return the marketplace provides you with a space to sell your goods.

In the on-line version, the space provided includes the shopping cart, check out and e-payment technologies. You are given a way to sell your goods safely and securely, as well as a place to display the items

145

for sale. An on-line marketplace will not typically have services available for you to tie in an inventory database. This type of solution generally only works well if you are selling a smaller number of items.

Amazon is the best known marketplace and is also one of the largest in terms of the number of businesses that sell through its marketplace. The other huge name in third party marketplaces is eBay. One of the biggest advantages with using either of these bigger companies is that they offer some tools to put your inventory database into your market "stall." Of course there are many others. Two of the well-known marketplaces for small businesses that make handmade goods are Etsy and ArtFire. These sites provide user friendly options that are easy to use. In the long run, it is usually more economical buy than to develop your own commerce solution. But in many ways, the choice between buying/building your own e-commerce solution and using a third party marketplace is like the choice between leasing or buying a building for your office. Each business will be best served by a different solution.

ALTERNATE PAYMENT SCHEME TECHNOLOGIES

In the past, people were suspicious about paying for items on-line. Fear of fraud, identity theft, or just plain stealing meant that e-commerce was slow to take off. Most of that is in the past now as credit card companies will protect on-line purchases just like those bought in a store. With that hurdle overcome, people are willing to embrace even more electronic forms of payments. They are paying using third party systems such as PayPal, paying by cell phone – the possibilities are almost endless!

ELECTRONIC PAYMENTS

Almost every business needs to be able to handle electronic payments. In the discussion that follows we're thinking only about the technology and process flows and not the commercial risk and legal implications, all of which a business must consider. We'll look at three different types of commonly used or up-and-coming electronic payment technology:

- Card payments
- e-Payments
- Smartphone payments

We won't discuss bank wires, drafts and letters, or other electronic payments that are typically only associated with financial institutions

CARD PAYMENTS

Credit and debit cards have been around a long time and it is assumed that many people and businesses are familiar with them. Credit and debit cards operate on the basis that somebody offers a card for payment and it is swiped through a type of electronic reader. Whether the reader is directly cabled into a PC or till or wirelessly connected as a stand-alone device, the process is the same. The cardholder will key in their PIN (personal identification number) and the PC or system will connect to the card providing company to check if the card has been reported stolen. If not, it will then check if sufficient credit or other balance is available to honor the transaction. If funds are available, the money will be transferred into the company's account with the card provider. If there are insufficient funds the transaction will be rejected

---

WARNING!

Card payments are one area where fraud is not uncommon. These frauds are frequently not connected to technology and are therefore outside the scope of this book. They include issues such as buyers making false claims of non-receipt of goods and obtaining their money back from the credit card companies (this is often called "chargeback) as a result. Many of these crooks specialize in targeting new Internet businesses that they believe are likely to lack business savvy. Any business that is new to accepting on-line payments should take detailed advice from their service provider about reducing and/or eliminating the risks of this type of fraud.

E-PAYMENTS

The e-payment is a variation of the card payment. This usually works on the basis of email IDs and the service is provided by one of several specialist intermediary companies of whom PayPal is perhaps the best known. With e-payments, the buyer (your customer) has an account with the e-payment service company and sends funds to that company via their credit card or bank. When the buyer chooses to pay for something on your site, the service company (such as PayPal) will confirm to the business's shopping cart package that the funds have been received.

At this point you can draw the funds down into your bank account whenever you wish. Of course you need an account with the service provider as well! By providing a "button" and auto-link from a web site directly to these specialist companies, a company can offer their clients a variety of payment methods. These services will take a percentage of the transaction as their fee. Just like credit cards, e-payment service providers have also gained customer trust by reimbursing people who have lost money in on-line payments due to fraud. As a result, more and more customers are feeling comfortable with using e-payments.

While PayPal is the largest and best known of the available e-payment service providers, there are others that are just as reliable. HyperWallet is a similar service geared towards Canadians but is also available in the U.S. Moneybookers provides e-payment services that are geared towards the UK market. While your business may deal in US dollars, remember that you are now reaching a global customer base! Versatility in payment options will make customers more apt to spend their money on your site.

SMARTPHONE PAYMENTS

Smartphones are especially suitable for on-line payment systems. They run on several different types of networks – GPRS, EDGE and 3G cellular phone networks, and Bluetooth and wireless Ethernet LAN networks. By setting up your ecommerce infrastructure properly, you can allow smartphones to make payments and receive receipts, just like any PC or laptop. This is the newest payment technology and is still not fully available in North America. In Japan, however, almost every vending machine will accept electronic payments from a smartphone – the cost of the item is simply added to the person's cell phone bill at the end of the month. The customer simply "calls" the vending machine with an SMS order. Another version allows smartphones to interact with the vending machine through wireless technology to pay for the item. And in Europe and some parts of Africa, travelers can pay for train and plane tickets on-line with their smartphone. The ticket is sent to the phone and the traveler simply holds up the screen of the phone to be scanned when they are ready to board! Keep these ideas in mind as you start to develop your e-commerce solution. These are the payment schemes that will be used more and more in the very near future.

THE CRITICALITY OF YOUR WEB INFRASTRUCTURE

The importance of security for your e-commerce solution cannot be stressed enough. It should always be one of the first things you think of when you are deciding what payment features to design into your website. Getting expert advice on setting up a payment system is crucial – because all it takes is a slight drop in your customer's confidence to put your business in peril. Some background on what systems are necessary for a successful e-commerce solution is useful. As a business owner, you have to ensure three aspects:

- Web browser compatibility with your website – If some people cannot use your website properly, they can't spend their money there.
- An adequate network setup – Is your setup designed to handle the amount of traffic your website will see?
- Security – Because this can't be stressed enough. You should always be thinking about the security of your website.

Remember, you should not worry about getting these details right yourself – that is what the experts are for. With this level of information however, you know the questions to ask when contracting these services.

INTERNET BROWSERS

Everyone is familiar with internet browsers, also called web browsers. A web browser is a software application that allows on-line users to view text, images, video, and anything else on a web page. More importantly for you, the web browser is the program your customer will use to purchase items from your website.

The most popular browser is Internet Explorer. Internet Explorer comes with full Microsoft support, and is already on any computer with Microsoft Windows installed. Mozilla Firefox version 3 is the second most popular browser available. These two web browsers will be used by over 85% of the customers who will view your site. Three other browses you may hear about are Apple's Safari, Opera, and Google's Chrome. As a business owner, you should not care which browser a customer uses on your site – you should expect that they all work. But that may not be necessarily true.

While there are standards in the computer language (HTML) that is used to make websites, not all browsers follow the same standards! A site that looks and works perfectly in Microsoft Explorer 7 may not work properly under Firefox – or even Microsoft Explorer 6! When implementing an e-commerce solution, make sure that your provider is testing the website design with all types of browsers. You do not want to lose a customer because the "click to buy" button does not show up properly.

THE IMPORTANCE OF YOUR NETWORK

We discussed networks earlier, outlining how they are a necessary technology component for any small business. But also we need to talk a little bit about your network in relation to an e-commerce solution on your website.

First, speed is crucial. Your network connection to the rest of the world (your bandwidth) needs to be high enough so that customers are not left staring at a slowly loading web page for minutes. This is the wide area network (WAN) part of your network. It can be thought of as your connection to the Internet. Secondly, keep in mind that all of the e-commerce information coming from the Internet will have to flow through the rest of your local network. Again, you have to make sure that your customers are not sitting and waiting on their side of the web browser for your order tracking database inside your LAN to finish sending data out. Thirdly, you want to have networking equipment that keeps track of how the data is flowing through your Internet connection and the rest of the LAN while protecting your local LAN from Internet issues. This type of "security appliance" can get quite expensive, but a properly set up network does not necessarily need the most expensive security appliance. This infrastructure is something you will have to discuss with the expert you have brought in to set up your e-commerce solution.

SECURITY

The importance of computer and network security for an e-commerce website cannot be overstated. A computer virus, or even obtaining an unwanted software program, can cause huge disruptions in your ability to do on-line business – in some cases even permanent destruction of data.

As discussed earlier, every PC in your business should be running anti-virus software, even those that are not involved with the e-commerce website. Think of two people in a room that has strong locks, making it safe and sound. If person two gets the flu and brings it into the room, person one can catch that virus as well, even if they never leave the safe, locked room. The same is true for your website server (the safe computer) and all the other computers in your business. Other basic protection for every computer is a firewall and an anti-virus program.

The next step is to ensure the security of each on-line transaction between your website and the customer's web browser. Encryption provides one of the best defenses against computer security threats and all the browsers mentioned in the previous section support data encryption. Data encryption simply prevents somebody from "listening in" on the exchange of credit card or e-payment information between you and the customer. The data is sent through the internet in a coded form that is very difficult to decrypt. While encryption is an important part of on-line security, it is primarily used by web servers to provide protection. Individual users can rely on firewalls to take control over their own web security. A firewall filters information from the Internet before it is received by the PC or network. Most operating systems have built-in firewall protections.

The final piece is physical security for your e-commerce computers within your office. These machines should only be accessible to a few people and kept in a very secure room. Once again, expert help to determine the appropriate security needs for your e-commerce solution is absolutely essential.

Summary

Having your business on-line isn't just about a new way to advertise your business anymore. It is more like opening up a new store in a really big city! So many "brick-and-mortar" stores that traditionally sold all their products through physical stores now sell over half of their goods on-line. And with the technologies available today, there is literally no business so small that it cannot take advantage of selling its products and services on-line. The key to using the technologies discussed in this chapter, as a new medium through which to do business, is to embrace the idea that they are not just a fad or a minor part of your business. Give these new mediums the same thought and analysis that you give any other new business process that you would implement for your business. They should not be discounted simply because you cannot see the benefit at first glance.

CHAPTER 7

EMERGING AND FUTURE TECHNOLOGIES - THE WORLD CHANGES

I n any book covering technology, this is the section that is often the most difficult to write. That's because guessing the future is a dangerous business and it is very easy to make wrong predictions. Innovations come and go very quickly. Nevertheless, having some thoughts about what technologies may be just over the horizon is certainly useful in helping businesses think ahead. At a minimum, just thinking ahead in terms of technology and your business, put you that much further ahead of your competitors. So, here we go!

VOICE RECOGNITION TECHNOLOGY

Some technology experts admit to being baffled as to why this technology has not made more progress and become more widespread than it has. As far back as the early 1980's, many technology prophets were predicting that the keyboard would disappear within 10 years. But as we can all see from the evidence around us, they were not even close. The reason why this has not occurred is fairly clear. Speech recognition is not as easy as it sounds. It has proven to be very difficult to get true and fully flexible voice recognition systems to work. But a lot of progress has been made and there are now some good, if limited, speech recognition systems around. Examples include voice activated car phone systems, voice prompted GPS systems, and some voice dictation systems that exist in word processing packages. Ever faster progress in this area seems likely and this is being driven in part by the increased availability of the very small hand-held devices outlined in earlier chapters.

Although these devices are now phenomenally powerful, many of them are already about as small as they can possibly be, while still providing the mandatory keyboard, touch screen or key pad necessary to use. Even with current models, it is not unusual to see people with larger fingers struggling to use the stylus or depress an individual tiny key on the keyboard or screen. It is difficult to see how these devices can be made much smaller due to the limitations imposed by the size of the human finger. Voice systems are the logical successor and this will drive the domain forward. The main issue with voice recognition systems that businesses will struggle with is the fact that one is actually talking out loud. Trade secrets, confidential information, and the inconvenience to others around you make any potential use limited to mostly private interactions.

UNLIMITED BANDWIDTHS – VIDEO TECHNOLOGY

Although the position has changed beyond all recognition in the early years of the 21st century, there still remain several inhibitors to the mass use of video conferencing and video communications. Those "vid-phones" so beloved of science fiction over 80 or more years, have never really arrived or made an impact in the mass market. There are several reasons for this but the most significant is the fact that video transmissions are large in size and very demanding in terms of data "traffic." For many years, it has been difficult to transmit videos over existing cable networks and get an acceptable speed and picture resolution – those jerky and fuzzy pictures with voice and image out of synch are a result of that lack of data transfer speed. In other words, they lack the bandwidth.

In the past there wasn't really much that a business could do to overcome this, apart from installing either special point to point cabling or using very high specification wireless or satellite systems. In both cases the costs were prohibitive for small businesses. But today many cable companies are expanding their systems and laying new fiber optic cables that offer massively expanded bandwidths. The increase in wireless frequencies and technology, coupled with improved compression techniques (the amount of space a signal takes up), mean that these services will become increasingly viable over the Internet and through ISPs. Sites such as Skype, Microsoft Live Messenger and LinkedIn are taking advantage of the increased bandwidth to provide acceptable video conference services. The images still tend to be somewhat jerky and of questionable quality, but there is definite progress being made.

CONVERGENCE OF HAND-HELD DEVICES

As outlined in previous chapters, this process is already underway. Currently, many products marketed as a "smartphone" or "palm organizer" or "hand-held PC" already offer a variety of functions, so that such a description does them little justice – and in some cases is a legacy of history. It seems likely that this process will gather pace and that there will be a selection of hand held PCs that will offer telephony, full web access, a personal organizer, camera and data device, while still being powerful enough to provide office software tools. There will no doubt be numerous manufacturers and product names/types – but no longer will a small business need to worry about the differences between a PDA and a smartphone. Every device will be able to do everything!

ROBOTICS

For decades industrial robots have been used in large scale manufacturing. As technology has become smaller and designs more sophisticated, there are signs that small business-sized (in both price and dimensions) robots could finally appear. No longer will they be the preserve of toy or model enthusiasts – they will spread into even the smallest businesses and into homes. There is no reason why small businesses will not be able to use robots in some components of their manufacturing in the near future. Rather than having to send items away to be built in a large factory far away, you could simply upload the design into your local robotic "factory." There is also the very real possibility of robots working in stores, like taking a customer order, assembling items in a bag, and then processing the payment. It is very possible and perhaps even likely that this area of technology will boom in the years ahead as there is a tremendous amount of research and development being done there.

BIOMETRICS

These techniques involve technology that recognizes aspects of our bodies that make us uniquely identifiable – fingerprints, retina patterns, faces, and perhaps rather further away, our DNA. This technology is already here and in use, though for the most part it continues to be in the domain of high security for large corporate enterprises, primarily because it remains somewhat unproven and very expensive. However, all the signs are that this will change. As the technology improves, suppliers will look to commoditize the solutions and roll them out to interested mass markets, including the small business. Nobody is suggesting that every small business would install retinal scanning systems on their office doors.

But perhaps their valuable and highly theft vulnerable hand-held devices for field staff could be protected by such technology. The device would simply refuse to work for anyone other than the assigned owner. Some PCs are already using fingerprint or voice identification and this seems to be something that will expand tremendously across many areas of technology in the years ahead. It could signify the end of the password!

The only security risk to consider is that while you may never divulge a password that sits in your head, it is quite possible that you or one of your employees will be forced to put your finger on that scanner that recognizes your print.

RFID (Radio Frequency Identification)

This is a form of radio chip that can be embedded into an object permanently or slipped in and removed in similar fashion to a bookmark. The basic concept is that this allows goods or vehicles to be tracked and identified as part of inventory control or delivery confirmation. In many respects it is similar to the well known bar coding technology but operates via radio transmissions and reception. This technology is already used in large business and is going to expand rapidly. It is also being used as a way to pay at drive through coffee shops and gas stations – simply wave your card at the scanner and payment is collected. Now imagine if someone can buy something at your business by simply walking out the door. The RFID tag in the item would be recognized by the door scanner and the customers RFID enabled card would be billed for the item.

Worldwide Interoperability for Microwave Access (WiMAX)

A new wireless standard that is currently gaining popularity is WiMAX, which has bandwidths comparable to "wired" internet connections. WiMAX can transmit data over a larger area and at faster rates than current standard wireless transmissions. Because it can accommodate various forms of data transmission, including VoIP, WiMAX may prove to be the future for business wireless. However, as much as hope is there that this technology catches on, it can still suffer from a few issues including periodic disconnections.

Cloud Computing

Prior to the early 1980s, most computing "on-line" consisted of boxes that had comparatively little power or "intelligence" connected to a central large computer called a mainframe. This mainframe provided all the programs and facilities used by the people connected to it. The PC from the early 1980s onwards changed all that.

Increasingly, computing power and function moved away from the mainframe to PCs and servers – known as "desktop" computing as all the computing power was sitting right there on your desktop.

Now with the expansion of PCs linked together through the Internet, some companies have developed a concept called "Cloud Computing," where the "cloud" roughly refers to the Internet, which harks back to the mainframe style of computing. In this concept, companies will provide "services" (which could be programs, media services and so on) across the Internet. The services are tailored specifically to the user's needs. In other words, much of the processing and "power" has moved off the PC owner's desk and back to a central machine or machines located elsewhere. This may have real advantages for some businesses, particularly as we see more and more smartphones and netbooks being used that are not as powerful as desktop PCs or even laptops. With cloud computing, they no longer need to be.

FOLDABLE PAPER-THIN SCREENS

Most offices have limited space and the PC's screen takes up a large part of the average desk. When not in use the screen is "dead space" that can be a nuisance in some circumstances. Already, there are paper-thin foils that are capable of displaying TV images and these can be rolled-up in a similar fashion to a newspaper. Although this technology is still new and still only available in the laboratory, it seems likely that it will be perfected and hit the market in the next few years. This isn't just a novelty.

The idea of a screen that can be lifted off a desk and "folded away" into the desk drawer will be attractive to many. What about a screen that can be tacked to the wall above your desk? It also opens up vast possibilities in the area of customer presentations. Carrying large screens to customers' sites is not very practical, so imagine the advantages of one that can be unfurled from a small briefcase! It could become a relatively decent alternative to carrying a portable projector for those must do face to face meetings.

THE END OF CABLES

For decades, "the dreaded cable" has plagued technology. The tangle of wires and cables between devices and their connection ports has caused many an accident and often looks unsightly. The advent of wireless technologies such as Bluetooth may mean that this jungle of cables is finally consigned to the history books within the next few years. However, technology experts have been promising the end of cables for years – but hope springs eternal!

INTEGRATION OF HARDWARE SYSTEMS

Already the advent of television shows provided over the Internet, coupled with home entertainment systems running through PCs, has shown that it is not necessary to have multiple "boxes" in the home with each one doing different things. Just as with hand-helds, technology is converging in the home. This consolidation has already become apparent in areas such as the fax/printer/scanner all-in-one devices. And there is now telephone over the internet services such as VoIP where it is possible to make and receive phone calls from your PC while you work. Using LAN and WAN technology, the future may involve far fewer individual boxes in the office. TV, radio, information systems, presentations, telephone, video conferencing and even on-line movies are all going to be delivered through one set on the desk-top. The technology is already proven and in use in big companies. It will be used in small companies in the immediate future.

INTELLIGENT & EXPERT SYSTEMS

Artificial Intelligence is a charged subject for many. Leaving aside the philosophical questions about what constitutes intelligence, universities and labs have been experimenting for decades with systems that can learn and adjust their behavior. There are some differences between the similar concepts of artificial intelligence and expert systems, but for the moment we'll consider that they're the same thing. Most of this area of technology has made little impact in business systems. Even where it has made an impact, remains to some extent, the domain of big business and large defense industries. This seems ripe for change in the years ahead as computer processing power continues to double every two years or so, as it has been doing for over 50 years.

It is likely that many business areas, notably application software, may start to see the increasing use of these approaches. Examples of this could perhaps be the expert system that deals with all incoming emails to the company, assigning priorities and responding to some automatically. The same system could answer incoming calls and route the call to the appropriate person based upon asking the caller questions. Unlike current systems that rely on the caller pressing a button or giving single word specific answers, expert systems may well be able to understand much free-form human speech and respond to many inquiry calls themselves.

REDUCTION IN PAPER

In an earlier discussion, we mentioned how paper continues to play a large part in the daily life of many businesses in spite of 50 year's of efforts to eliminate it where possible. Although it has been wrongly predicted many times before, the rapid growth in the Internet, e-commerce and low cost technology is highly likely to drive a huge reduction in the usage of paper in business. As more and more businesses conduct their activities electronically, both with other businesses and with their customers, the need for paperwork will rapidly diminish. Paperwork and paper usage will be seen as being prohibitively expensive and, in some cases, environmentally questionable.

Not only will the need for paper communications and engagements decline but, more importantly, the ability of customers, suppliers and other businesses to actually process paper transactions will reduce. Those small businesses that continue to insist that their customers engage with them via written order forms and check payments, are going to find life increasingly difficult.

Always Connected

Cell phones are everywhere these days. In fact in many countries in Europe, Africa and Asia there are more cell phones than landlines. Cities all over the U.S. are installing free wireless Internet that anyone with a laptop, handheld, or smartphone can use. Everywhere you go these days, you can communicate wirelessly. It won't be long now before we will be able to stay connected to the Internet, twenty four hours a day and seven days a week, no matter where we go. Some people eagerly await the day this will happen. These are the people who are already addicted to their Blackberries or who are constantly using twitter from their iPhones. Some people live in dread of when they will never be able to get away from technology. A week hiking in the furthest reaches of the Appalachian Mountains could be interrupted by an urgent email from work. But whether you long for or fear the days of being always connected on-line, make no mistake that they are coming. For the small business, this will offer an unprecedented opportunity to maintain an "office" that could span the globe. When distances begin to mean absolutely nothing in terms of communication, a small business suddenly has as much chance of getting that new contract in Bangalore as any big company does. You will be face to face with the entire world.

Everything Connected

The fact that you can have your email messages read out to your answering service is a great wonder to some people. Now how about your fridge telling your smartphone that it is almost out of milk – which then tells your car to plot a route to the closest convenience store? Or how about a printer at your office that notifies your inventory database that it is almost out of ink? Or imagine that your garbage bins can register that they are almost full and send a message to your smartphone that will remind you to contact the maintenance service company for your building. These ideas start to sound a little farfetched, but in the years to come, more and more of our electronics will be designed to interact and communicate through the internet both with you and with each other. As all of our electronics get "smarter" in terms of sensors and communication technologies, we will find more and more ways to automate all of their functions. So things that we once had to take care of ourselves, such as remembering to buy more ink cartridges for the printer, will be taken care of automatically by the printer itself. Now that is efficiency. Of course, you will then have to get the webcam to spy on the printer to make sure that it doesn't order more cartridges than it needs...

INCREASED COMPUTER POWER

Finally, the big one! In terms of power, storage capacity and functional capabilities, the modern PC and hand held device is unrecognizable from their predecessors of 10 years ago. Even so, as many small businesses know, the desperate cry of "The computer is SLOW!" is still heard regularly. One could have heard the same complaints 30 or 40 years ago when the only "on-line" computer usage was through large terminals connected to mainframe computers. That's happening because the moment a manufacturer builds a new and faster PC with the latest and fastest processing chips inside, the companies writing the software for them simply make their products larger, more complex and more resource demanding. Frequently the extra power available through the new PC is just gobbled up by new versions of the software that most businesses know and love such as Windows, Microsoft Office and so on. Some people complain that some of their programs now take longer to run than they did five years ago even though the PC today is ten times more powerful than the one they had five years back. It's possible that in some cases they may be right!

The limitations of existing computing power are, to some extent, holding back some areas of technology. A PC running video conferencing, Internet searches and an accounting package at the same time can find itself grinding to a halt fairly quickly. Coming along is something called quantum computing. It's still experimental, but it means building processing power at the atomic level rather than on silicon chips. It isn't going to arrive in business computing for years, but when it does it offers the prospect of unlimited computing power. Gone forever will be (or should be) the cries of "It's seized up!"

PART II

BUSINESS TECHNOLOGY CONSIDERATIONS

CHAPTER 8

OUTSOURCING BUSINESS TECHNOLOGY

This book has stressed many times that technology need not be seen as complicated when considering its use in a midsize or small business. Nevertheless, it is a fact that some businesses feel there is danger in getting so caught up with integrating technology in their operations that they lose sight of their core business activities. Sometimes expressions along the lines of "we are an XYZ company, not a technology operation!" may be heard. Even if these perceptions are rarely entirely accurate, it is understandable that some small businesses really do not want to think about technology very much – they just want to use it. For companies that do not have the time or staff to take on even a moderate learning curve of technology and its application, there is a solution. It's called outsourcing.

Any small business can have access to systems of phenomenal sophistication that deliver major benefit, yet all that can be seen in their premises are a few PCs, a printer or two and perhaps a PBX. That's because they have taken up the services of an external technology supplier that provides all the complex applications and environment for them. So there are no servers, no backups, no mirror site arrangements to administer, no software upgrades to worry about and so on. This is all taken care of for them by a third-party. Outsourcing as an option for the development and maintenance of a business technology environment has been around a long time, although it has spiked tremendously in the last decade. There are a large number of companies offering various types of outsourcing services that vary by customer requirement and, as a result, price.

In terms of describing a typical outsourced arrangement, consider a small business with five employees. Each employee has her own PC that is attached via a small LAN and telecoms link to the outsourcing company. From each of these PCs the user can access and run their core application systems such as general ledger or payroll. The fact that these programs and databases happen to sit on a server in the outsourcing site many miles away (sometimes on another continent!) is entirely transparent to the users. They can also access their web site, deal with e-commerce transactions and function entirely in the same fashion, as if all the equipment and software sat in their own office.

THE PROS AND CONS OF OUTSOURCING

Using an outsourcing company can offer major advantages – but as always, there are some issues to consider. Let's examine some of the pros and cons, starting with the positives.

THE PROS

LATEST TECHNOLOGY

Technology changes rapidly. Trying to keep a technology environment "up to date" can prove expensive. Not only is this the case when purchasing initially, but in the case of hardware and software, there will be "upgrades" and fixes released that need to be installed. This can be time consuming and slightly intimidating if a company is not fully conversant with the technology concerned. This should not apply in the case of many outsourcing companies. One of the selling points of their services is usually "access to the latest technology" so they are motivated to keep it up to date and fully maintained. This can be a big responsibility for some small businesses and having it all taken care of by somebody else can be an attractive option.

SPACE SAVING & WIRES

Technology is getting ever smaller and wireless may be replacing many forms of cable connections, but even so, more powerful boxes needed for e-commerce or large database technologies can be bulky. The accompanying wires are tangles that many offices would prefer to do without. At least some of these can be removed to the outsourcing company's site.

RISK REDUCTION

Previously I described the need for small businesses to make regular backups, run test "restores" to simulate a disaster, and possibly maintain a "mirror" standby site. An outsourcing company can provide all of these things as part of the deal. The overall risk reduction and the removal of worry and responsibility this provides for a small business should not be underestimated.

THE AVAILABILITY OF EXPERTISE

Any outsourcing company must accept full responsibility for the support of the environment on their own premises. That means that if they have a problem, they are responsible for fixing it. As part of the contractual and commercial discussions with a potential client, they should also offer what's called a Service Level Agreement (SLA). The SLA should define what services they guarantee and within what period. We will come back to this later, but it is relevant here because the SLA should stipulate, amongst other things, the provider's availability. This is important to any client because it confirms the minimum average hours and times (usually expressed as a percentage) that the service will be available. So if the small business wants a guaranteed 90% availability during business hours seven days a week, then this needs to be clearly written into the SLA. Whatever it takes in terms of support expertise to meet that level is then provided by the outsourcing company. It's worth noting that the higher the availability demand, the higher the cost may be in some cases. It's also worth being pragmatic. Few suppliers of technology services can guarantee 100% availability 24/7. Some companies providing these services will also offer, for a cost, on-site support of the small business's technology such as their PCs and printer. This may be worth considering.

A REDUCTION IN THE NEED FOR ON-SITE TECHNICAL EXPERTISE

Once much of the technology responsibility has been passed via contract to a service provider of this type, the need for a business to engage in training and expertise development of their own staff should be greatly reduced. This can reduce costs and allow people to focus on their core responsibilities rather than also being a part-time technology guru. This doesn't mean that a "zero knowledge" situation is achievable or desirable for the small business. Most business-to-business communication today involves a degree of familiarity with technology – such as "Could I link directly to your ordering system?" It will make such dialog much easier if at least some basic familiarity with modern technology is still in your business.

THE CONS

COST

Unsurprisingly, people who provide technology outsourcing services expect to make a profit. The cost of some outsourcing arrangements can be high depending upon requirements for things such as availability.

DEPENDENCE CULTURE

There is a fine line between outsourcing one's needs to a service provider of this type, and becoming exclusively dependent upon them for all technology matters. It's worth remembering that the outsourcing company's priority and work schedules are not necessarily those of the small business. In a situation where a small business has their technology and expertise in-house, the small business can adjust their priorities as needed if they need to make changes to facilitate a new business stream. If the technology is outsourced, this now becomes a process of negotiation and, possibly, extra costs as the outsourcing company's time to participate in the discussions will need to be paid for, unless of course this was already anticipated and therefore stipulated in the contract.

THE "CAPTIVE CLIENT" SYNDROME

Things in business change. It may be that for the past several years having an outsourced technology operation was fine. But now for one reason or another, the small business wishes to bring their technology back in-house or perhaps move it to another service provider. It's not unusual at this point to discover that co-operation from the existing provider can suddenly become a little "sticky" and perhaps not what it should be. There is an old saying in technology that "outsourcing is easy – bringing it back in house is much trickier." It is a fact of life that enthusiastically supporting activities that are going to result in the loss of a client is unlikely to be high up the priority list of any such service provider. Many difficulties, complexities and costs may be encountered en-route.

A "YESTERDAY'S NEWS" CLIENT

In all aspects of commercial life, a client is never more popular and worthy of first-class service than in the run-up to the final signing of a contract. It's not unusual after that to see a reduction in attention and sometimes service from a service provider. This can also be true for technology outsourcing. Once a service provider "has" the client and their business, it is not easy for the client to simply say at a later date "I want out" in the event of unsatisfactory service. In some providers this can, at times, generate an attitude of complacency towards their client base and an associated reduction in customer service standards.

PRICE HIKES

From time to time one encounters businesses complaining that while the initial cost of the service was attractive, over time the contract was subject to several price hikes of an unreasonable amount. Although this practice is rare, it can happen. The way to avoid this is to use a component of the contract – once again we'll come back to this.

LEGAL ISSUES

As is the case with many businesses, sometimes a client has highly sensitive information that it stores in their PC files and databases. In some cases, U.S. or International law may limit the company's freedom to pass this information on to a third party's systems – such as the servers of an outsourcing company in another country. This is a complicated area to discuss. If the small business has any legal concerns at all about outsourcing, then independent professional advice should be taken from a lawyer specializing in these areas.

THE SLA & CONTRACT

The service level agreement (SLA) and contract between a small business and a technology outsourcing company can be both a pro and a con, depending on how well the SLA is written. It is a negative in the sense that it can take a great deal of time to get right and it can be a bureaucratic and legalistic nightmare. But it is essential that this is taken seriously because it is perhaps the one time the business has the opportunity to apply real leverage to the service provider. Remember, the small business's negotiating power will never be greater than in the period before the contract is signed. NEVER sign the contract before there is a full SLA in place signed by the service provider, and that fully meets your business needs. The achievement of an appropriate SLA & contract is a serious subject and should be approached with much respect. What we will do for the purpose of enlightenment is examine some key concepts and areas that should be carefully thought about and addressed in the contract and/or the SLA:

Cost Containment

Focusing on the start up and first year's cost is fine. But as mentioned earlier, unless a 50% increase per annum is acceptable, the extent to which the supplier can increase their service costs per year should be constrained by wording in the contract.

Right Of Orderly Exit

It is always worth ensuring that the contract legally obliges the service provider to support fully and efficiently, any future move away from their services to another provider or a return to in-house services.

Current Technology

Make sure that the contract obliges the provider to keep their software and technology up to date.

Security

The contract should contain cast-iron guarantees that any information stored at the provider's premises is secure and will not be passed onto any third-parties without the written consent of the small business in advance.

Service Availability

Be certain that this matches your business operations requirements.

Reciprocal Pain

One issue with many SLAs is that although they guarantee a service level, they do not say very much about what will happen if the service provider does not achieve the minimum service level. If the small business's systems are unavailable for one or two days, then the pain and cost to the small business is usually clear – lost revenue and lost customers. Nice as a sincere written apology from the service provider is, it costs them nothing. Make sure that the service provider underpins their service availability guarantees with a final commitment to share the pain, in the event it does not meet its undertakings.

Disaster Recovery & Standby

In theory the service provider and the contract should provide this as a routine matter, but it always pays to make sure it is documented!

Specification of Support

The price of the contract should include a defined amount of specified telephone or perhaps on-site support that the provider will make available. It is imperative that this is clearly sufficient from the small business's point of view and if necessary, expanded upon. The reason for this is simple. If the service provider's contract says "unlimited telephone support in the event of a problem", this may sound phenomenally generous. But in practice it could mean that every call to them of a "how do I do xyz?" would be chargeable as it is advice and *not* problem support. Don't get caught out by wordplay like this – check it in detail!

AREAS IN OUTSOURCING TO CONSIDER

As we discussed previously, you do not have to outsource your entire technology infrastructure. While there are gains to be had in getting one company to provide everything for you, there are also positives to keeping control of all the technology portions that you are comfortable in maintaining yourself. For now, we'll assume that you may only want to outsource some aspects to reduce the number of employee work hours spent on technology issues. The following are some areas that, if outsourced, can save a lot of time for your company and can be cost effective to outsource.

MAINTENANCE & REPAIR OF PCS

Computers require maintenance and repair often enough that it can be aggravating as a small business owner to be constantly dealing with the hassles. The lifespan of the average computer remains about two to five years – some peripherals such as printers may not even survive that long. Rather than dealing with the expense and struggle of repairing and maintaining your office PCs and peripherals, you can outsource the entire issue by either leasing the equipment from a provider or signing a maintenance contract for all the equipment in your office. While not strictly outsourcing, the leasing concept is the same. The leasing company will own the computers sitting on everyone's desks. They will be responsible for setting up the computer, providing the basic software on it, and providing a replacement if a computer breaks. The same sort of agreement can be made for printers, video projectors and other peripherals. The advantage here is that the service provider has to ensure that all your desktop PCs are working – and if you need another computer for a new employee, it is usually quite simple to call the service company and have another computer added to the contract. A maintenance contract provides essentially the same services except that you own the equipment – and would have to provide the funds to buy a replacement item when something breaks. The maintenance contract simply supplies the expertise of somebody coming in to do the physical repair or replacement. When looking at the cost of a maintenance or leasing contract, business owners should factor the cost of PC replacements, upgrades, repairs and lost time into deciding whether outsourcing maintenance is worthwhile.

APPLICATION DELIVERY

Rather than paying for and installing all the software for employee's PCs, more companies are instead paying a company to provide that software over the Internet. Application service providers (ASP) offer access to various software programs over the Internet for businesses to use. The ASP owns the software, which it operates via its own server. ASP can provide single, specialized software programs such as credit card processing or standard document processing software programs that all of your employees use. Almost any software you would run locally can also be outsourced from an ASP. Some ASPs will even provide the hardware to run the software on, providing you with a server on site so that the software can run over your local LAN instead of over the internet. Of course, this will generally be a more expensive option. Using ASPs can save your business money since you do not need to acquire software licenses nor spend the money on required upgrades. And with the software comes comprehensive support, which includes disaster recovery and data backup services in many cases. Some ASPs now provide a model called software as a service (or SaaS). It is sometimes called on-demand software, since the applications are based on a pay as you go model. Web conferencing is an excellent example of the SaaS model now available. If the software is not something your business uses on a regular basis, an ASP which provides software using this model will be a less expensive option. Whether you go with a SaaS or a standard delivery model for outsourced software, make sure that the software is what you need, not just what the ASP wants to sell you. Also understand how you (or potentially your customers) can access the software and the implementation requirements.

PAYROLL

Outsourcing payroll needs has in the past, been more for large companies than the average midsize or small business. That has changed and now payroll services can be an economical way for the small business to offload this activity. Payroll services are responsible for all aspects of processing employee payments. You simply provide wage and hour information for each employee, which the service provider then uses to calculate withholdings and other deductions. The payroll service can also print and mail checks directly to employees, or they can electronically deposit them into the employee's bank account. They will also provide support for tax filings, mailing the appropriate documents and communicating with the IRS if necessary. Many payroll services offer the added benefit of on-line logins, which allows business owners to view payment histories and other records of financial transactions at any time over the Internet. The greatest advantage of using a payroll service is that it allows you as the business owner to focus on growing your business, rather than worrying about the intricacies of accounting. However, outsourcing payroll is generally not going to be an economical option for small businesses with fewer than 10 or 15 employees.

SUMMARY

Outsourcing offers potentially numerous advantages for the small business, but it cannot be approached and undertaken on a "drop this in their lap and run" basis. The inter-relationships here between the technical, legal and commercial issues can be complicated. It may be advisable to approach an unbiased expert in this area to manage the initial outsourcing for you. Outsourcing is just one option in dealing with the technology of small business – it is not going to be the right choice for everyone. But do not discount it simply because of horror stories you may have heard or because you think the cost will be too high. Sometimes outsourcing your technology operations really is the most cost effective option.

CHAPTER 9

DELIVERING BENEFIT & AVOIDING RISKS

L ittle in life is risk free. Buying and using technology is no different. Many large corporations have written off literally billions of dollars in failed technology projects, so mistakes and risks are not restricted to smaller businesses. When one reads the history of these technology catastrophes in major companies – and the Internet is full of examples – it is hard not to be struck by one over-arching fact that comes out of every post-mortem on the disasters. The companies concerned had quite simply got lost in the glamour of the new technology.

There is no universally agreed on list of prioritized "good practice steps" to help reduce risk and achieve benefit. The order of importance will vary by company and situation. However we can pick out some obvious things to always keep in mind and highlight others to think about.

Don't Automate Bad Systems

One of the oldest sayings in the computer industry is:

"Automating bad ideas doesn't make good ideas – it just makes bad ideas faster."

When considering new technology, particularly in the area of internal core or customer facing applications, you have a perfect opportunity to have a long, hard think about how you are operating the business processes in that area. This is an absolutely necessary first step because over a period of time, it is commonplace for sub-optimal processes to evolve and find their way into work practices. These are usually explained and justified on the basis of "we've always done it that way."

Whether the application package covers accounts, CRM, stock control or any other area, most computer systems are now sufficiently flexible to do things the way you want them to. If existing poor methods are just automated "as is" into the new system, then real business benefits may be difficult to obtain. Therefore, if you are changing software or computer systems, consider a full review of your business process as well!

GREAT TECHNOLOGY DOES NOT MAKE A GREAT BUSINESS

Sometimes businesses express disappointment that although the new technology is successfully installed, it hasn't led to customers pouring in the door – or whatever the originally projected benefits were. There are many reasons this can happen, but one of the most common is that the business has lost sight of the fact that at the highest level, a business must have a sound business idea that the market wants. Technology can help in the delivery of that idea but it can't correct a flawed one. To put it bluntly, if a small business is trying to sell a product or service that nobody wants, then technology cannot solve the problem!

CONSIDER ALL NEW TECHNOLOGY AS A FORMAL

PROJECT

A very common mistake made by many businesses, big and small, is to assume that technology can be purchased "off the shelf" and then just plugged in. This is true in a few simple cases such as buying a new printer. But in general terms, it is a dangerous assumption to make. When purchasing even a small device such as a smartphone, there are frequently issues to be considered concerning integration with existing systems and usability. The issues may be small, but are unlikely to solve themselves. Those issues need to be managed.

Also, it is not usually a good idea to ask the business's accountant or one of the general office staff to oversee the implementation of the technology within their normal workday. They will be forced to try to make it all happen in a few spare minutes here and there, squeezing the time out of their already presumably busy schedules. This is likely to result in a piece of potentially useful hardware or software sitting on a shelf unused or only used at 20% of its capabilities.

Whether the purchase is as large as a complete WAN/LAN setup with video conferencing, or as small as in the case of buying a new laptop, make sure it is taken seriously and that somebody is in charge as "project leader" and held accountable for making the purchase happen successfully. Allow the project leader time to do the job properly and ensure that appropriate technical expertise is called in to support them when necessary. If it is important to do for the business then do it right!

AVOID "BIG BANG" IMPLEMENTATIONS

If installing several new modules of technology, it is a good idea to avoid putting them in all at the same time and switching them all on in a "grand opening ceremony". This implementation approach is called "big bang" and if it works it can be spectacular. If it doesn't work (which happens much more often), it can cause more than just embarrassment! When changing, upgrading or implementing technology, one is effectively changing many variables in the technology environment. If something goes wrong and everything stops working, it can be very difficult to diagnose the problem – you have many things to troubleshoot instead of just one. Therefore, as a method of reducing risk and aiding problem diagnosis, keep changes small, discrete and incremental – one step at a time! Just do not have the project extended to multiple years if it can be avoided.

AVOID LENGTHY PROJECT IMPLEMENTATIONS

One of the deadly technology implementation issues many big businesses face is the multi-year, multi-phase project. By the time implementation is done, the technology is old and the original business opportunity lost. Then the cycle begins again while other more nimble businesses are moving onto the advanced business technology capabilities. Of course there are circumstances that make the multi year project unavoidable. However, too many businesses accept far too easily, that projects must continue into infinity. Your objective is to get it in fast and move on!

AVOID "DEAD END" TECHNOLOGY

This can be a tricky one. Many technology professionals have predicted at times that a given device, communications protocol or software package would prove to be the standard of the years ahead – only to be subsequently proven totally wrong. In practice, this is becoming less of a risk than it was in the past. Many systems, hardware and software, are now complying with open standards that makes them much more "future proof" than earlier generations of the same systems.

Even so, no company wants to find that they are stuck with systems that can't be linked to other, newer systems or devices in the immediate future. The only real answer to this is to speak to several independent technology experts to get their opinions and conduct some of your own market research. Remember that the person selling the solution is unlikely to be unbiased!

BEWARE "STATE-OF-THE-ART" TECHNOLOGY

Technology that is entirely new to the market with little or no proven track record may make a company the envy of their competitors – but it can also be a little risky. If purchasing technology that has just come out of the lab, there will always be quirks and flaws that you have to work out with the company who made the product. But if the launch of the product has fallen flat in the marketplace six months afterwards, it can start to become very difficult to get service and support. No one invests their time in a failing product.

THINK SUPPORT, INSTALLATION COMMITMENT AND LEGALLY BINDING CONTRACTS

This subject isn't too important when purchasing a printer or perhaps a standalone video projector, but it becomes very important when purchasing larger value packages of equipment or just about any software application system. If the technology is installed successfully, then it should quickly become incorporated into the business and become an important part of daily operations. If one day the technology goes "crunch!" and stops working, then the effects could prove to be at best a serious inconvenience and at worst a show-stopper for the business. In these situations, having fast access to skilled staff capable of resolving the problem is critical. This is not the time for the business to discover that no support is available, or that it is available only on the second Tuesday of each month, or that it is readily available but only at a cost of $350 per hour.

Technology doesn't always obligingly plug in and start to work immediately. Installation, configuration and integration with existing systems are all key challenges with most types of technology. Having the world's most sophisticated video conferencing system in the office won't count for much if it doesn't work. It can be even more frustrating when the supplier walks off saying something like "It's not our system it must be your WAN" or "Our product is fine, but you need to buy the XYZ software for it to run on your server."

In general, it is always advisable to clarify what implementation or post-implementation support will be available as part of the purchase. If the supplier states something that sounds acceptable, make sure it is confirmed in a legally binding contract. It's also usually worth trying to get the supplier to confirm that their product or software will work in the technical environment that's already in place. In the case of ISPs, it's important to remember one thing when discussing reliability. It doesn't matter how much you have spent building your website and e-commerce facilities – if the ISP server they sit on isn't up and running, then your website is inaccessible and effectively useless. Most ISPs have excellent availability statistics and are happy to share them with potential customers. But if there is an offer that looks too good to be true and it is coupled with an absence of availability statistics, then it is sensible to be cautious and look elsewhere!

UNDERSTAND THE TOTAL COST PROJECTIONS

Any new technology that a business buys will usually have four costs associated with it:

The purchase cost
The cost associated with the price tag of the product.

The consequential costs
In other words, does the purchase of product "x" at a price of 1000 dollars also mean the business will have to buy, from other companies, products "y" and "z" (or take upgrades)? And if so, how much will they cost?

The installation cost
The cost, if applicable, of hiring technical expertise to install the new purchase and make it work.

The ownership cost
This is the annual cost of running the new purchase. In the case of software or communications infrastructure this may include annual license fees or communication traffic costs.

It is not unusual to find that companies understand the first point above very well. But the following three are sometimes overlooked in the drive to get the new product or system into the business. For example, a business may use an ISP that provides a package for their web site services, based upon a certain cost per month. The business then decides to purchase a software product that it uses regularly. It requires frequent large database up and downloads from the software provider's website. This will increase the data traffic across the ISP's link, which may then incur additional monthly charges from the ISP to the business.

MAKE SURE THE SOLUTION IS SCALABLE

This subject is not quite as important as it once was due to the increasing compatibility and standardization of many types of technology. Even so, it is worth ensuring that any technology purchased today is capable of growing and expanding as the company grows and expands. Areas such as storage are not usually a problem as additional DVDs, CDs, hard disks and flash memory such as USB drives are all readily available at a low cost.

Areas that may require some thought in this respect arise in ISP services, network bandwidths, server capacity and database sizes in some application software. All these may be purchased and configured initially based upon assumptions relating to the size of the business. If the assumptions are exceeded, there can be cost implications or, more rarely, significant upgrade costs.

Once again, this subject should be explored in advance with the technology supplier(s) and their responses verified through an independent expert or similar source.

DON'T STINT ON TRAINING

One of the most common reasons for technology failing to deliver anticipated benefits is that the people using it have been insufficiently trained.

The business world is tough and budgets are constrained, particularly for small businesses. It is always tempting to reduce costs by not paying for that training session originally envisaged – after all, can't the people using it just read the manuals? Do not give in to this siren-call.

Sometimes, in the case of relatively simple technology such as a smartphone, it may be possible to understand the product and learn how to use it by flicking through a manual. If the technology is more complicated this solution will not work. Also, the people using the new technology may not find learning via reading to be a particularly successful strategy for them.

This is particularly important in situations where applications technology is being purchased. Giving someone a small hand-held device for web browsing and saying, "away you go" may not be a major problem. Giving them new accounting software and a manual and saying "away you go" is likely to yield little except a frustrated employee and bad financial data. Appropriate training is never wasted money, especially when you are dealing with business technology.

DON'T DAMAGE YOUR REPUTATION

Keep in mind that there are some dangers in letting your web site go "live" before the web site has any significant content. Many potential clients or even casual browsers may feel peeved if they have taken the effort to go into the site only to find it consists solely of one page saying "site under construction" or a photograph of the business owner waving amicably and saying "coming soon folks."

Most business people and potential customers don't find that sort of thing amusing and it should be avoided at all costs. Don't make a start-up web site so basic that your business is questionable. Make sure that even if it is described as "basic" that it still gives someone visiting it *some* value relating to the business operation. An absolute minimum should be some business contact information and a page describing the business and what the customer can expect from the website in the near future.

INCLINE TOWARDS "BRAND" SOLUTIONS

There was once a saying in the computing industry that "nobody ever got fired for choosing IBM products." That sentiment is debatable in terms of accuracy, but the basic principle that the risks of failure and disappointment are usually (though not always!) lower with known or prestige makers than newcomers, still holds true.

Looking at PCs as an example, you will see a price range that varies by specification of the PC as one would expect. Even when looking at PCs of very similar specification, there are often price differences based upon whether or not the manufacturer is well known. It is a sometimes controversial view, but if a company has been in the market for some years and built market share plus brand name recognition, then that alone usually proves they are doing some things right! Across much of the spectrum of technology, there is something to be said for looking to established and well known companies for solutions if one wishes to minimize risk. This doesn't mean they are the best or the right choice, technologically speaking, or that they necessarily offer the best customer service. But it should be factored in, especially if you have a very low risk tolerance. Most likely they'll still be around in twelve months time if you're having trouble and need help.

USE CONSULTANTS

Another cost of new technology that is frequently eliminated very quickly as costs add up on a new technology purchase is the cost of hiring experts for pre-purchase advice, guidance and implementation support. Paradoxically, a blank check is often available for the same service once a catastrophe has arisen! Every business must ruthlessly control its costs. But in a situation where it is contemplating a large purchase on complicated technology, forgoing the use of an expert to advise, guide and consult is a truly risky false economy decision to make.

Some businesses believe that such expertise can be obtained from the Internet, the suppliers or the next-door neighbor's 15 year old kid who is something of a whiz with computers. The dangers of taking input and advice exclusively from a supplier or vendor have already been touched on (they are unlikely to be unbiased). The other two sources may be fine if one is contemplating a $50 purchase of a printer. But these "unofficial experts" are likely to offer inadequate risk reduction reassurance for a business contemplating spending $10,000 on new technology infrastructure.

Few vendors will offer refunds to a business because it has purchased the wrong solution. So make sure in advance that the right solution has been selected and be prepared to pay for this reassurance if necessary.

MEASURE THE BENEFITS

Most companies perform some form of cost-benefit analysis before they commit to a purchase. This is good discipline, but it's only part of the story. It's not unknown for benefits to look good on paper, but then fail to materialize. This is rarely a technology issue but is more commonly associated with a reluctance of people to change their culture and operations as originally planned. This means opportunities are lost. Make sure someone is accountable for measuring the benefits achieved to ensure they are realized!

FORCE USE OF THE TECHNOLOGY

To drive the maximum benefit from a technology investment, it has to be fully utilized in accordance with the initial plans and designs. Achieving this is not always easy and sometimes takes a little courage. As an example, a business installs an on-line ordering system for its clients' use to reduce paperwork and administration. But the clients refuse to use the new system and keep phoning orders in instead.

Theoretically this should not happen. If the system is good enough, it will offer clients advantages over the old phone or fax system and their use of those communication channels should wither away naturally. Unfortunately, life is not always that simple and all people, customers or not, can be constrained by habit. In this scenario, the on-line customer ordering system may end up being in place side by side with the old method it was meant to replace – a veritable catastrophe in terms of cost-benefit and efficiency.

In such cases, it may be necessary to "force" use of the new system by subtle methods (price incentives) or to even switch off the old way of doing things. This is where the courage comes in!

Don't Forget Insurance

This book can't go into the sometimes horrifically complicated world of business insurance, but it can offer a basic reminder – accidents happen! Somebody moving a desk may put a leg through that brand new (and expensive!) plasma projection screen. Someone else, while moving the central application server, drops it and now the internals consist mainly of splinters. A sales representative calls to say they've accidentally tipped their laptop into a pond. These things happen. If the advice given earlier in the book regarding backups and standby systems is followed these catastrophes need not stop a business dead. But they can cause serious expense, particularly for a small business, unless appropriate insurance coverage is in place.

Summary

In this chapter we've given some advice about reducing the risks of buying and using technology. Throughout the book we have explained the best ways to think about how to implement those new technologies. Now it is time to put all our knowledge to work for us. We'll look at some common small business scenarios and see just how technology can help those businesses to grow, to become more efficient, and to reach more customers.

Business Technology

CHAPTER 10

APPLYING TECHNOLOGY TO YOUR BUSINESS

Earlier we stated that each business's needs and opportunities are different and must be considered individually. This remains true, but there are also certain things that most small businesses would do well to consider as a minimum in order to survive and prosper. The following list below describes the bare minimum technology infrastructure for the 21st century:

MINIMUM BUSINESS TECHNOLOGY

- Computers:
  - o One (or more) desktop PCs
- Support for hardcopies:
  - o Printer
  - o Copier
  - o Scanner
  - o Fax machine
  - o Shredder
- Security:
  - o Effective PC and wider network security software such as firewalls and anti-virus

- o Individual PC security via locks and passwords
- Contingency & Peace of Mind
  - o An Uninterruptable Power Supply (UPS) to avoid the chaos that can result if there is a local power outage
  - o A method of backing up the databases and critical information stored on the PCs (and a proven method of restoring them quickly)
  - o A secure off-site location where the backups are stored (or copied)
  - o A disaster recovery plan for "worst case scenario" situations
- Communications
  - o A PBX for managing voice communications and fax transmissions
  - o Connection to the Internet provided by an ISP so that the business can "get out" and customers/suppliers can "get in"
- Application Systems & Internal Core Processes
  - o An "office suite" that provides basic office administration support for things such as word processing, spreadsheet usage, some desk top publishing and simple database building

Let's look at this minimum set of technology in a real world scenario: a one-person watch repair business.

SCENARIO ONE: A ONE-PERSON, NON-COMPLEX BUSINESS

In this first scenario, we'll examine a very simple operation using our hypothetical watch repairer as the base. In this business, the owner has a small main street shop that specializes in watch and clock repairs. Customers bring pieces in to the front of the shop to be fixed. In the rear, the business owner has a small office and workshop. At the moment he or she has more business than they can handle and has no need to advertise for more. All customer and supplier transactions are face to face and payments are via cash or check only.

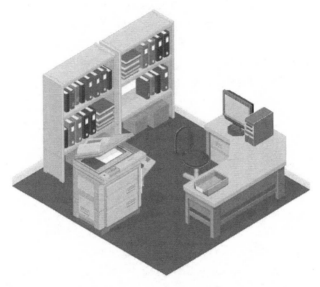

FIGURE 10.1 A single person setup is relatively straightforward

In this simplest of 21st century business examples, the business owner may be able to survive and even prosper but requires at minimum, some very limited technology capability. In this very simple model, the watch repairer has the technology capability to:

- Run core function applications such as tax and customer record systems, invoices, recording payments and writing documents
- Print invoices for customers, send or receive faxes, and scan in documents received for electronic filing
- Make and receive conventional landline telephone calls
- Access the Internet to find rare parts, check for specialist suppliers and send and receive emails

The components needed to achieve this basic "entry level" technology are simple and relatively low cost. These are all technologies purchased at local retail stores or available from many local providers. If there is one key message to take from this first "landscape", it is that all these components are part of the construction of a basic technology infrastructure. All of these components are required whether a business is small or large. They are all fundamental building blocks that can be expanded and built upon as a business grows and its needs change.

SCALING UP TO A WEB-CAPABLE BUSINESS

Although the "one person" business is common, it is not the norm. Most businesses have more than one person working for them and multiple PCs. They may also market their services. The next step up, both in size of technology and amount of technology required, is a small business with a few employees that wants a "web presence." This automatically implies that the business also needs some type of advertising on-line as a way to drive customers to its website.

With a larger reliance on technology, this level of business needs to worry more about ensuring that its technology is always running smoothly. This means a better level of technical support for the technology, both in-house and through service agreements. The following, along with the minimum technology described in scenario one, becomes the required technology set for this level of small business.

- Computers:
  - A hand-held device and/or a laptop PC to support "out-of-office" activities (many very small businesses will use their laptop as their "desktop" PC)
- Contingency & Peace of Mind
  - A technical support agreement with an expert or experts
  - At least one but preferably two people who are trained to be "local experts" in the systems

- Communications
  - A LAN for connecting PCs and peripheral devices such as printers (wireless or wired)
  - A web camera (webcam) for video communications
  - A company web site
- Advertising
  - If not the same people as the point above, some access to web search ranking expertise
  - A visibility and business to business networking and showcasing presence through one of the many web sites dedicated to that function including sites such as MySpace, LinkedIn, Facebook, Twitter and so on
- e-Commerce
  - A method of linking the web site activities to the company's core application processes, i.e. "the back office."

Once again, we can look at this technology in action through a real world scenario.

SCENARIO TWO: THE REALTOR

FIGURE 10.2 The technology complexity increases with multiple locations

Let's consider another business, a small realty company. It has only one office, but employs a staff of five operating over two floors, with two of the employees spending significant time out of the office doing valuations. The company also advertises properties over the Internet and handles customer enquiries that are emailed to the company. In this scenario, the company will need the basic "technology infrastructure" from scenario one but the numbers will change. The business will need a few more laptops and desktops and most likely at least two printers, but the technology components will be the same.

The technology components that make this scenario different are there to meet the additional needs of the business. Since there are multiple PCs in the office, located on different floors, it makes sense to link them together via a LAN, so that they can share information. It may also mean that all staff in the office can share a single printer or fax from their PCs and a single connection point to the Internet. The other significant functional change here, in terms of business efficiency, is the need to "connect" staff working in the field to the office and the wider Internet.

THE NEED FOR AN ON-LINE PRESENCE

In this simple small business operation, the company is allowing the external world access to one of its applications, a summary of its property database available through the Internet. For this to work, the Realtor maintains a website for its business on the Internet. On this site, the Realtor stores a copy of its property database that it periodically updates to reflect new properties coming in and those that have been sold. The sophistication of this type of facility can vary from very simple to very complicated. As an example, potential buyers that visit the office in person may specify ideal requirements that they are looking for in a property. The staff member will note these and then search their files for matching properties.

Through the Realtor's web site this process is replicated, only this time automatically. The potential buyer specifies preferences by electronically "ticking boxes" indicating what type of property he/she is looking for. The website application then automatically finds and displays to potential buyers only those properties that meet their requirements. The processes are largely identical except that in one case the "sorting and selecting" is done automatically rather than by a member of staff. The Realtor has developed its customer facing technology in the form of a website and used the opportunity to create a new medium in which to do business.

INCREASING STAFF AVAILABILITY WITH TECHNOLOGY

Few businesses would think about trying to operate without telephones. In the 21st century this is generally taken to include some form of cell phone. Technology in this area, however, has changed beyond recognition in the past five to ten years. And with that change has come the expectation by both employers and customers that employees be available via email and voice at all times.

Considering again our realtor scenario, let's assume that a client on site is a rare "hot prospect" for a sale in a depressed market. But the client asks a question about the property that the representative can't answer, although she knows that the information needed is stored on the company web site. In such a scenario, what sounds better to the potential buyer?

- *"Sorry, can't help you with that one."*
- *"Sorry, I don't know, but you can look it up later yourself on our web site!"*
- *"I am trying to get the office to look that up now but they're engaged and I've left a message – they'll get back to me eventually, I hope."*
- *"I'm not sure but I'll look up our web site immediately and give you the answer in a minute or two."*

We know that the first three options are at best, undesirable and, at worst, unacceptable. The fourth option is the best of the group, but the Realtor will need to equip its field staff with either a laptop PC that can attach to the Internet via a wireless connection or a hand-held device that can act as an Internet access point.

There is nothing wrong with the laptop route and that may be adequate in many situations, however they are largish boxes and usually need to be used on a desk and perhaps with a chair – things that may not be readily available on a building site or in a green field environment. So our Realtor decides to equip its field staff with smartphones capable of accessing the Internet anywhere cell phone service is available.

The days are gone when someone out of the office had to be written off as "out" and contactable only by cell phone. Through the utilization of modern communications techniques and with the new powerful and integrated hand held devices, the person out of the office is now really an extension of the office in another place. Let's take a look at an example of just how well this can work.

A TYPICAL DAY FOR THE REALTOR'S STAFF MEMBER

In the morning, a staff member has a client viewing and happens to arrive onsite a few minutes early. From her car she connects to the home office's systems to download the administrator's changes to her daily schedule. Her diary is now fully up to date. Still having a few minutes to spare, she uses her smartphone to download and read any emails that she would normally have dealt with on her PC had she been in the office. She quickly responds to those that are urgent.

She then uses her smartphone to call the client's cell phone for a status check and finds he is only one minute away. The client arrives and they look around the property. During the viewing the client questions something on the company's web site and the representative immediately uses the same handheld to access the Internet, allowing the client to browse the company's web advertisement to check the detail he was confused about.

Eventually the client leaves and before the realtor locks up, she thinks that a view from the back of the house is particularly attractive and should be added to their web site advertisement. She uses her smartphone to photograph the view, then sends this image back to the office and asks the administrator to add it immediately to their web site advertisement. A few minutes later, as she gets into her car outside the property, she connects again to the Internet and brings up the company website. She sees to her satisfaction that the photograph she has just taken is already available for the whole world to see. All this technology exists today and is in use in similar ways.

THE PHYSICALLY GROWING SMALL BUSINESS

Once a small company starts to develop satellite offices to deal with increasing sales, more technology can be brought into play to make this transition work smoothly. A growing business can add the following technologies to its business at this point:

- Contingency & Peace of Mind
  - o A standby site

- Communications
  - o A wide area network (WAN) for connecting multiple office buildings together in a high speed network
  - o A web camera (webcam) that can be used for video communications

We can see the effectiveness of these technologies with a third scenario.

SCENARIO THREE: THE REALTOR EXPANDS

To examine the next level of technology capabilities, let's return to the example of our local friendly Realtor from scenario two. The company has done well and has expanded by opening an office on the other side of town to cater to different districts. This is working well on the whole, but they've had some problems with staff commuting between the two offices for meetings and getting caught up in traffic. Sometimes key documents needed in one office are found to be in another – meaning taxis and couriers shuttling back and forth in emergencies. Although none of these issues are catastrophic, they are a nuisance and an unnecessary cost.

WIDE AREA NETWORK

These types of problems can be overcome by linking the two offices with a WAN. The staff can share computer systems, re-route phone calls to each other, and even send hardcopy output to be printed on a printer in the other office's location. For many reasons a WAN may offer a small business significant advantages as part of an infrastructure component. It can be installed for moderate cost using a variety of technologies. The cost may be less than the amount you pay in terms of couriers, vehicles and lost employee time. And with a WAN in place the Realtor can take advantage of other technologies.

VIDEO CONFERENCING

In the case of the Realtor, the WAN coupled with video conferencing may well eliminate the time wasted in traffic by their personnel in transit from one office to the other. Using webcams, microphones, and VoIP, the two offices can conference with each other with all parties being able to see the others involved on their respective screens and monitors. At this point, the Realtor can setup a video conferencing system to contact large clients through its website. This could save even more money if the company's representatives can reduce the number of on-site visits they make to clients' offices.

STANDBY SITE

Once our Realtor has its two sites linked via a WAN, it also has the opportunity to set up a mirror of the company's data at each physical site. Once one has a second location securely connected by a WAN, it becomes possible to have "mirror images" of all key files automatically copied across the WAN every night to the other office. In the event of fire or flood that knocks out one building, this second office can immediately start up as the hub of the Realtor's operations with little or no loss of information or customer service potential. This is an example of the "hot standby" disaster recovery capability discussed earlier. When thinking about backups, mirror sites and disaster recovery, it's worth remembering that the storage available at the backup site must at least equal the amount of critical storage used at the primary site.

A FULLY INTEGRATED E-COMMERCE BUSINESS

Almost all businesses need a way of getting their customers to "come in", stay a while and browse what's on offer, and buy some "thing" or service. Once the customer has made a purchase, the business wants to be able to bill their customer and get the customer to pay. We now come to the last stage of business technology – a full e-commerce solution. This small business conducts some (or all) of its business transactions with customers and suppliers on-line. This is the model of small business that many companies will need to move towards in the years to come as more and more business is done over the internet. Integrating an e-commerce system with your business increases the number of required technologies:

- e-Commerce
  - o An e-Commerce presence
  - o A method of accepting and making electronic payments via credit card and bank transfer
- Application Systems – Internal Core Processes.
  - o A basic "Integrated business management" package that provides bookkeeping, payables, receivables, inventory management, product database and customer records or CRM capabilities (if possible these should all be capable of integration directly with the front-end e-commerce systems)

Let's dive into our last scenario to see just how these technologies are implemented.

SCENARIO 4: THE CANDLE MANUFACTURER

Let's use the example of a small manufacturer of scented candles and related items for our e-commerce scenario. To establish its business on the Internet and trade via e-commerce with the wider world, this company needs the basic technology infrastructure and application components from previous scenarios, plus the technologies outlined above. In principle the operation is little different from a conventional physical shop. A customer visits the web site and looks at what the candle making company is offering. If she likes an item she buys it and pays for it. The candle company then dispatches the product to the delivery address. This sounds easy, and it isn't difficult, but how can it be made to happen in an e-commerce way?

WEBSITE REQUIREMENTS

First, a web site has to be built. Many businesses prefer to hire the services of a software company that specializes in building web sites. A web development company develops the site, building in facilities such as catalog display and selection, a "shopping basket" and a "checkout" function. The website is set up so that it can access the company's candle database to provide descriptions and available quantities. After the candle company has a web site, it loads its product catalogue and prices onto it. It has a facility that allows customers to select items to buy and is now able to accept credit cards and PayPal transactions. Now the company is ready to accept on-line orders!

THE BACK OFFICE

Let's say the on-line part of our candle maker's business has been "live" for six months and things are going great! Customer numbers are shooting up and money and orders are pouring in. With its efficient web site and payment process in place, the "customer/sales" side of the business is working well. However, this causes problems for the back office because the internal accounting side can't keep pace. Worse, the company is spending more and more time administering the placing of orders with their raw materials suppliers. The back office process for dealing with the orders looks like this:

- Orders come in from the web site together with the customers' electronic payment

- The person responsible for customer orders updates the internal customer records system and passes details of the payment to:
  - o The accounts person who then posts the sales to the respective ledgers and books
  - o The order & customer administration person who sends a ship confirmation to:
    - ▪ The shipping person who retrieves candles from stock and ships to the customer, updating the stock records in the process

While all this is happening, the person that actually makes the candles keeps an eye on stocks of both completed candles and the raw materials for making them. When stocks of raw materials and candles are getting low, he orders new materials and makes more candles. This involves issuing orders to suppliers, chasing them for delivery, and notifying accounts that an order has been placed so that monies to pay are put aside (accrued). Once the supplier has delivered the raw materials, an invoice is sent to accounts which then goes through the process of bookkeeping and eventually provides payment based on the supplier's invoice.

The problem is that many of these business functions may not be automated. So in each case the process steps above will be made to happen by phone calls, pieces of paper, emails or meetings. All of these processes may work adequately – but in all probability they are slow, error-prone and labor intensive. As a result, it is probably expensive for the small business to operate. What's worse is that these slow processes will hinder the growth in sales that the e-commerce part of the business is now providing. Talk about wasted energy! The solution is for our candle manufacturer to implement an integrated business management technology solution.

INTEGRATED BUSINESS MANAGEMENT

The business decides that it needs to increase business efficiency by implementing an enterprise management package that will tie available stock and raw materials to incoming orders and automate some of the invoicing and materials ordering. Our company hires a consultant to help them to develop a new business process that fits with an automated sales and procurement model. Eventually, with the new system in place, the business process now looks like this:

- A customer places an order on the web site and pays for the items
- The system automatically updates the stock files
- Once the stock file reaches pre-set levels, the system automatically sends an order to the external suppliers for raw materials
- The system automatically makes an accrual entry into the company's accounting books
- The system automatically updates the customer's records and notifies the shipping department to take the order from stock and ship
- When external raw materials are delivered, the Receiving Manager updates the "raw materials" section of the stock file and the system automatically notifies accounts to pay the supplier

The above description does not have every single process step included. However the point of this outline model is to illustrate a critical difference in the efficiency of a small business with an integrated business management solution in place. In this model, the candle company has delegated the tasks of record keeping and updating to a relatively low cost PC system. Much of the basic routine process work, such as updating customer records or posting to account ledgers, is now all done automatically.

No longer does a highly skilled and expensive accounting professional have to spend a significant amount of her time posting updates to ledgers and reconciling. This is now all done automatically. No longer does the manufacturing unit have to engage in writing out orders and sending the invoices to their suppliers. That can be done automatically also. Now the accounting staff is free to concentrate on areas that demand their skills, such as customer queries, banking, tax reporting, short term investments and end of year accounting. The manufacturing area can concentrate on what they're good at – making candles.

CUSTOMER RELATIONSHIP MANAGEMENT

There is one other aspect of the scenario above that is missing, Customer Relationship Management (CRM). In the candle company's situation, they will quickly build a repository of information about customers. This is potentially of significant importance for future marketing – such as a mail-shot aimed at Christmas special offers. It can also be used for market trend analysis such as what customers and where are buying what types of product? While not a necessity for the business, CRM would help to grow sales even further without requiring more spending on advertising. By focusing instead on existing customers in very targeted ways through information in its CRM, our company can increase sales from existing customers while seeking out new potential customers.

SIMPLE INNOVATION WITH TECHNOLOGY – CASE STUDY

NYAMINGS

Nyamings is a little Thai restaurant that opened for business in 2006. After 2 years the business was doing relatively well. The food is excellent but the small size of the restaurant meant that people coming in either had to wait too long or they simply left if the restaurant was full. The owner discerned that while her customers like to come and eat, there was not much else that drew them there. She decided to reevaluate her business strategy to see where she could make any possible improvements.

After an assessment she determined that to evolve the business and to make it a solid destination point where customers were willing to lineup and wait for seats, and where every night open was a full night, she needed to do 2 very specific things.

1st: Re-brand the store as a top of the line restaurant where the cooking of the meal was part of the dining experience. To accomplish this she determined that opening up full visibility into the kitchen would create the exact atmosphere she was looking for and that making the kitchen a fully integrated part of the restaurant was a winner.

Solution: Install 8 large screen LCD monitors around the restaurant and 4 in the kitchen. Install and connect digital video cameras displaying the dining room in to the kitchen staff and the kitchen to the diners.

The results: Well you can guess. The patrons were treated to a unique dining experience while the kitchen staff and the chef became energized and motivated seeing their creations being thoroughly enjoyed as they work on new dishes.

2nd: Create a customer experience like none other in town, where every return customer would be known by name and along with their exact dining preferences and dining history.

Solution: Implement a simple CRM solution that is then used to track each and every paying customer of the restaurant.

- Document each customer's drinking, eating, seating, waiter preferences.
- Document every reservation made and kept/canceled by customers.
- Implement a face recognition software link to each documented customer in the CRM tool.

The Results: Every time that Peter Jackson enters the restaurant for dinner, the host/hostess of the night is able to welcome him by name.

"Hello Mr. Jackson, so nice to see you again. So sorry you weren't able to make it last month. Would you like the same table as your last visit or would you like something a little different. Can we get you a glass of that 25 year old GlenLivet?"

SUMMARY

In this chapter, you can see how many of the technologies outlined throughout this book can be applied in "real" situations – from a basic one PC/one person business to a moderately complicated e-commerce manufacturing and sales business. A genuine one-person operation will be able to do without some technology components, as in the case of our watch repairer example, but businesses of that type are becoming unusual. In particular, the e-commerce and e-advertising technologies are becoming more and more essential as increasing numbers of customers choose to shop and pay through the Internet. Hopefully you can see that today's technology can revolutionize the way a business operates, markets itself and, more importantly, the way it does business with its customers.

CHAPTER 11

TECHNOLOGY IS YOUR OYSTER

I n this book we have examined the reality of life today for a midsize and small business and concluded that, like it or not, an increased use and exploitation of technology is inevitable. We have shown that technology is nothing mysterious. It can be thought of in business terms such as external customer facing technologies, business efficiency technologies, and business medium technologies. We have also looked at some classic, if hypothetical business requirements and shown how technology can be used to significantly improve the way a small business functions – including mobile computing and telephony. We have also tried to provide a sense of some of the technology that is now on the horizon. We examined some specific scenarios and outlined some of the classic ways small businesses can incorporate technology in the world today. However, in the final analysis, is there an overall message to our various discussions and illustrations?

Until the late 19th century, businesses functioned perfectly well without electricity. In the first quarter of the 20th century, many businesses worked well without a telephone. Towards the middle of the century most businesses worked fine without faxes, electric typewriters and photocopiers. Even towards the earlier part of the final quarter of the 20th century, many businesses continued to prosper without any significant "computer support."

Yet at the change of each epoch, the ability for the above businesses to continue to survive reached virtually zero. Any business attempting to run on steam and candle or gas power alone in 1925 would have found it difficult to do so – the world had gone electric. A business operating in 1940 without access to a telephone would have struggled – the world of telecoms had arrived. A business in 1985 trying to prosper without a photocopier, electric typewriters, and complicated phone systems, telex and desk calculators would have had a major and probably insurmountable challenge – the age of the electric and even early electronic office had arrived. Today we have passed another threshold – the business technology age. It is here and the pre-technology ages have gone just as the steam age has.

CONQUERING TECHNOLOGY OBSTACLES

Most small businesses know this and look to participate and prosper, but they are inhibited by three main factors:

- Budgets
- Knowledge/fear
- Skepticism

In a book of this nature, it isn't possible to deal with each of these in any specific detail as they vary depending on the business and the set of circumstances. What can be said about each is this: In terms of budgets, can any small business afford not to take technology seriously and invest accordingly? The owner of the mill running on steam power in 1900 may have thought that an electrical power supply was an unaffordable luxury and decided to give it a pass. However shaky their finances were, could this ever have been the correct decision?

Technology costs have fallen dramatically in recent years. Technology spending for small businesses can be a relatively small component of their overall cost base when compared to people costs and raw materials/inventory. Somehow, the funding will need to be found. In terms of lack of knowledge and the fear that this can generate, these are easily overcome. Hopefully this book has already provided a basic grounding in business technology. This can be significantly expanded upon through Internet research, other books, journals and, most importantly, through duly qualified advice and guidance.

It is a fact that many business people were skeptical and even frightened when telephones first appeared. The first electronic calculators were considered by many to be far too complicated when compared to the traditional slide-rule. A lack of knowledge and the associated fear that comes with it should not stop the smaller businesses moving into the technological areas outlined in this book. If fear does rule, the medium term result for the business will be sadly predictable.

Skepticism is the hardest factor to overcome, because it is sometimes justified. Everybody knows stories of how technology has failed to deliver the business value on which it was sold. Delivering instead, headaches and disappointment to the businesses involved in these failures. And these stories are not just folk-tales. Of course there have been major technology disasters. It's also wise to apply a degree of healthy skepticism to some of the claims, thrown around, sometimes far too liberally, by some technology suppliers. Even so, this skepticism must not be allowed to cloud the basic business realities. Those realities are clear. For even the smallest of businesses, technology is now essential. With the right guidance, growing businesses can profit tremendously from technology readily available to them.

YOUR BUSINESS TECHNOLOGY FUTURE

It is hoped that this book has placed business technology in its business context and de-mystified much of the jargon surrounding it. If it has helped a midsize or small business to start thinking about how technology can improve its business, then it will have succeeded. If after reading this book you now consider leveraging an integrated business management solution, or fully outsourcing your technology environment to a managed services provider, I will consider this book successful. Your business technology strategy has started taking shape!

So what are the next steps for a midsize or small business that wants to know more? The answer can be given in one word – ASK! The future is bright for smaller businesses that show enthusiasm and interest in the use of technology to drive forward. If one of the main things holding your business back from exploring new business technology capabilities is a lack of knowledge, then the most important thing that you should take away from this book is that the knowledge you need is available all around you.

Experts, on-line, consultants, articles and books can provide the insight and information you need to successfully use technology to interact with your customers, to make your business more efficient, and to sell your goods and services through new mediums.

APPENDICES

APPENDIX A

RESOURCES

Following is a listing of sites for most of the technology categories reviewed in the book. There are a few things to note:

1. This resource list is a representative sample from the internet and while these sites are active at the time of the printing of the book, it is very likely that some will not function due to a variety of reasons (e.g. sites frequently restructure, changing URLs in the process).
2. Being listed here does not indicate recommendation or endorsement.
3. The sites are all listed in alphabetical order; therefore sequence is of no importance.
4. The list will be a combination of large companies with major products on the market for many years and small entrepreneurs and innovators trying to carve out a nice with smaller businesses.
5. The sites listed here is a mere subset of what is out there waiting for you. This list is to give you a starting point to minimise the time spent searching. Nothing is more frustrating than clicking thru 100s of sites only to find a few of relevance.
6. Enjoy!

ACCOUNTING

Bottom Line Accounting
http://www.bottomlineaccounting.net

Coda 2count
http://www.coda.com

CYMA Accounting
http://www.cyma.com

Data Pro Accounting
http://www.dpro.com

Denali Business Accounting
http://www.cougarmtn.com

Intuit QuickBooks Pro Edition
http://www.quickbooks.intuit.com

Microsoft® Office Accounting Express
http://www.ideawins.com

MYOB BusinessEssentials
http://www.myob-us.com

Peachtree Pro Accounting
http://www.peachtree.com

Simply Accounting
http://www.simplyaccounting.com

Smart Accountant
http://www.smart-accountant.com

SYSPRO
http://americas.syspro.com

BioMetrics

BioAccess
http://www.bioenabletech.com

Bio-Enterprise
http://www.axistech.com

BioScan Security
http://www.brsgrp.com/bio-scan-security.html

BioTrust
http://www.cogentsystems.com/BioTrust.asp

DaonEngine
http://www.daon.com/products/daonengine.html

DERMALOG Finger payment
http://www.dermalog.de/english/3/15/Bio-Payment.html

MorphoFace Investigate
http://www.morpho.com/MorphoTrak/Morpho/morpho.asp

Precise Match-on-Card
http://www.precisebiometrics.com

Blogs

Blogger.com
http://www.blogger.com

Live Journal
http://www.livejournal.com

Live Spaces
http://home.spaces.live.com

Social Go
http://www.socialgo.com

Traction
http://traction.tractionsoftware.com/traction

Tumblr
http://www.tumblr.com

TypePad
http://www.typepad.com

Vox
http://www.vox.com

WordPress.com
http://wordpress.com

Xanga
http://www.xanga.com

BUSINESS INTELLIGENCE

MicroStrategy
http://www.microstrategy.com/Products-Services

Actuate BIRT Interactive Viewer
http://www.actuate.com/home

IBM Cognos Business Intelligence
http://www.cognos.com

InetSoft Style Intelligence
http://www.inetsoft.com/products/StyleIntelligence

Logi 9
http://www.logixml.com

QlikView
http://www.qlikview.com

SAP BUSINESSOBJECTS
http://www.sap.com/solutions/sapbusinessobjects/index.epx

SAS Business Intelligence
http://www.sas.com/technologies/bi/index.html

Tableau Desktop
http://www.tableausoftware.com/products/desktop

BUSINESS PROCESS MANAGEMENT

Adeptia BPM Server
http://www.adeptia.com

BizFlow
http://www.handysoft.com

BPM Suite
http://www-01.ibm.com/software/info/bpm/offerings.html

Business Process Management Suite
http://www.appian.com/bpm-software.jsp

Lombardi Blueprint
http://www.lombardisoftware.com/bpm-blueprint-features.php

Oracle BPM Suite
http://www.oracle.com/technologies/bpm/bpm-suite.html

Process360
http://www.global360.com/products/bpm/process360

ProcessMaker
http://www.processmaker.com

Savvion BusinessManager
http://www.savvion.com/business_manager

SmartBPM
http://www.pega.com/products

TIBCO BPM
http://www.tibco.com/software/business-process-management

CLOUD COMPUTING

Elastra Enterprise Cloud Server
http://elastra.com/products/elastra-enterprise-cloud-server

Cohesiveft
http://www.cohesiveft.com

Dell
http://www.dell.com/cloudcomputing

Eucalyptus
http://www.eucalyptus.com

FlexiScale
http://www.flexiscale.com

IBM Cloud Labs
http://www.ibm.com/ibm/cloud/labs

RackSpace Cloud
http://www.mosso.com/cloudservers.jsp

RightScale Cloud Management Platform
http://www.rightscale.com

Force.com
http://www.salesforce.com/platform/sites

StrataScale
http://www.stratascale.com/home

Sun
http://www.sun.com/solutions/cloudcomputing

COLLABORATION

Basecamp
http://www.basecamphq.com

Beehive Collaboration
http://www.oracle.com/technology/products/beehive

CentralDesktop
http://www.centraldesktop.com

ConcourseSuite
http://www.concursive.com/products.shtml

DeskAway
http://www.deskaway.com

Eloops
http://www.eloops.com

Groupswim
http://groupswim.com

Huddle
http://www.huddle.net

Lotus Domino
http://www-01.ibm.com/software/lotus/products/domino

Mindquarry
http://www.mindquarry.com

Novell Groupwise
http://www.novell.com/products/groupwise

Octopz
http://www.octopz.com

ProjectSpaces
http://www.projectspaces.com

Sharepoint
http://www.sharepoint.com

CUSTOMER RELATIONSHIP MANAGEMENT (CRM)

CenterBase
http://www.centerbase.com

CLPSuite
http://www.clpsuite.com

Maximizer CRM
http://www.maximizer.com

Microsoft Dynamics CRM
http://www.microsoft.com/dynamics/default.mspx

RightNow CRM
Suite http://www.rightnow.com

Sage CRM Solutions
http://www.sagecrmsolutions.com

salesforce.com
http://www.salesforce.com/crm/products.jsp

Siebel CRM
http://www.oracle.com/applications/crm/siebel

Sugar
http://www.sugarcrm.com/crm

Zoho CRM
http://crm.zoho.com/crm/login.sas

DATA BACKUP

iBackup
http://www.ibackup.com

Carbonite
http://www.carbonite.com

vaultLogix
http://www.dataprotection.com

Data Deposit Box
http://www.datadepositbox.com

Mozy
http://www.mozy.com

Dakota Backup
http://www.dakotabackup.com

3X Sytems
http://www.3x.com

ElephantDrive
http://www.elephantdrive.com

NovoSoft Backup
http://www.remotedatabackup.net

Diino
http://www.diino.com

RhinoBack
http://www.rhinoback.com

TekVault
http://tekvault.onlinebackupsolution.com

SugarSync
https://www.sugarsync.com

DOCUMENT MANAGEMENT

ArkWorks
http://www.ark-works.com

Captaris Alchemy
http://www.captaris.com/alchemy

Content Central
http://www.ademero.com

Document Locator
http://www.documentlocator.com

Documentum
http://www.documentum.com

DocuXplorer Professional
http://www.docuxplorer.com

Dokmee Professional
http://www.dokmee.net

FileHold Express
http://www.filehold.com

Globodox
http://www.itaz.com

ImageNow
http://www.imagenow.com

infoRouter
http://www.inforouter.com

KnowledgeTree
http://www.knowledgetree.com/products

Laserfiche Document Management Systems
http://www.laserfiche.com

Questys Solutions Document Management System
http://www.questyssolutions.com

ERP or Integrated Business Management

Enterprise 21 ERP software
http://www.tgiltd.com/

Everest® Advanced
http://www.everestsoftwareinc.com/index.asp

Glovia Solutions
http://www.glovia.com

Intuitive ERP
http://www.intuitivemfg.com

Microsoft Dynamics GP
http://www.microsoft.com/dynamics/default.mspx

NetSuite
http://www.netsuite.com/portal/home.shtml

Oracle Ebusiness Suite
http://www.oracle.com/applications/e-business-suite.html

Sage Mas 500
http://www.sagemas.com/

Sage Pro ERP
http://www.sageproerp.com/

SAP Business One
http://www.sap.com/smallbusiness/solutions/overview

HR/Workforce Management

Ascentis HR
http://www.ascentis.com

Authoria
http://www.authoria.com

Checkpoint
http://www.checkpointhr.com

Halogen
http://www.halogensoftware.com

HRsmart
http://www.hrsmart.com

iemployee
http://www.iemployee.com

Kronos
http://www.kronos.com

OrangeHRM
http://www.orangehrm.com

PerfectHR
http://www.perfectsoftware.com

SilkRoad
http://www.silkroad.com

Success Factors
http://www.successfactors.com

UltiPro
http://www.ultimatesoftware.com

Internet Service Providers (ISP)

CenturyTel
https://www.centurytel.com

Charter
http://www.charter.com/Visitors/Home.aspx

Clearwire
http://www.clearwire.com

Comcast
http://www.comcast.com

EarthLink
http://www.earthlink.net

EMBARQ
http://www.embarq.com

HughesNet
http://www.hughesnet.com

Juno
http://www.juno.com

LocalNet
http://www.localnet.com

Mediacom Online
http://www.mediacomcc.com/internet_online.html

NetZero
http://www.netzero.net

Optimum Online
http://www.optimum.com/online

Qwest
http://www.qwest.com

Verizon
http://www.verizon.com

Windstream
http://www.windstream.com

OFFICE TOOLS/SUITE

Ability V5
http://www.asiability.com

Corel WordPerfect Office
http://www.corel.com

Easy Office
http://easyofficepremium.com

FlySuite
http://www.flysuite.com

Google Docs
http://docs.google.com

IBM Lotus Symphony
http://symphony.lotus.com

iWork
http://www.apple.com/iwork

Kingsoft Office
http://www.kingsoftresearch.com

Office Professional
http://office.microsoft.com

OpenOffice.org
http://www.openoffice.org

StarOffice
http://www.sun.com/software/staroffice

ThinkFree Online
http://product.thinkfree.com/office

Zoho
http://www.zoho.com

ONLINE E-MALLS

Shops of Web
http://www.shopsofweb.com

Ace Shopping Mall
http://www.aceshoppingmall.com

Amazon
http://webstore.amazon.com

ebay
http://stores.shop.ebay.com/_stores/hub

First Stop Shops
http://www.firststopshops.com

GLC Mall
http://www.goldleafcrafters.com

Go shopping
http://goshopping.com

Main Street Mall Online
http://mainstreetmallonline.com

Point&Shop's online shopping mall
http://www.pointshop.com

PAYROLL SYSTEMS

ADP PayForce
http://www.adp.com

Intuit Payroll
http://payroll.intuit.com

Online Payroll Services
https://www.paycycle.com/external/home.jsp

Paychex's Online Payroll
http://www.paychex.com

PayWindow Payroll System
http://www.zpay.com

PenSoft Payroll
http://www.pensoft.com

PerfectPayroll
http://www.perfectpayroll.com

Perquest
http://www.perquest.com

Saral PayPack
http://www.saralpaypack.com

SurePayroll
http://www.surepayroll.com

PC Maintenance (Cleanup, Defrag, etc)

Advanced System Optimizer
http://www.systweak.com/aso

Norton Utilities
http://www.symantec.com/norton/norton-utilities

PCTools
http://www.pctools.com

Super Utilities
http://www.superlogix.net

System LifeGuard 2
http://www.systemlifeguard.com

System Mechanic
http://www.iolo.com

SystemSuite
http://www.avanquest.com/USA/pc-utilities

TuneUp Utilities 2009
http://www.tune-up.com/products/tuneup-utilities

WinCleaner OneClick
http://www.wincleaner.com

RFID

Active RFID
http://www.wavetrend.net/default.aspx

Alien
http://www.alientechnology.com

Confidex
http://www.confidex.fi

GAO RFID
http://www.gaorfid.com

Intermec
http://www.intermec.com

RFID Global
http://www.rfidglobal.org

TagsysRFID
http://www.tagsysrfid.com

Zebra
http://www.rfid.zebra.com

SECURITY (SPAM, ANTIVIRUS, ETC)

AVG Internet Security
http://www.avg.com

233

BitDefender Internet Security
http://www.bitdefender.com

BullGuard Internet Security
http://www.bullguard.com

CA Internet Security Suite
http://shop.ca.com

ESET Smart Security
http://www.eset.com

Kaspersky Internet Security
http://usa.kaspersky.com

McAfee Internet Security software
http://home.mcafee.com

Norton 360
http://www.symantec.com

Panda Internet Security
http://www.pandasecurity.com

Steganos Internet Security
http://www.steganos.com

Trend Micro Internet Security
http://www.trendmicro.com

Webroot Internet Security Essentials
http://www.webroot.com

ZONEALARM Internet Security Suite
http://www.zonealarm.com

SHOPPING CARTS

1ShoppingCart Pro
http://www.1shoppingcart.com

3DCart
http://www.3dcart.com

AmeriCommerce
http://www.americommerce.com

AspDotNetStorefront
http://www.aspdotnetstorefront.com

Coded Software
http://www.csecommerce.com/home.htm

CrownCart
http://www.crowncart.com

Interspire
http://www.interspire.com/shoppingcart

livecart
http://www.livecart.com

Pinnacle Cart
http://www.pinnaclecart.com

Volusion
http://www.volusion.com

Zen Cart
http://www.zen-cart.com

Znode
http://www.znode.com

SOCIAL NETWORKING SITES

Facebook
http://www.facebook.com

Flickr
http://www.flickr.com

FriendFeed
http://www.friendfeed.com

Friendster
http://www.friendster.com

hi5 Networks
http://hi5.com

LinkedIn
http://www.linkedin.com

LivingSocial
http://www.livingsocial.com

Multiply
http://multiply.com

MySpace.com
http://www.myspace.com

Reddit
http://www.reddit.com

SodaHead
http://www.sodahead.com

Twitter
http://www.twitter.com

Vimeo
http://www.vimeo.com

Yelp
http://www.yelp.com

YouTube
http://www.youtube.com

WEB CONFERENCING

Acrobat Connect Professional
http://www.adobe.com/products/acrobatconnectpro

Citrix GoToMeeting
https://www2.gotomeeting.com

iMeeting
http://www.ilinc.com

InstantPresenter
http://www.instantpresenter.com

InterCall
http://www.intercall.com

MegaMeeting
http://www.megameeting.com

Microsoft Office Live Meeting
http://office.microsoft.com

Nefsis
http://www.nefsis.com

Netviewermeet
http://www.netviewer.net

Web Conferencing
http://www.web-conferencing-central.com

WebEx MeetMeNow
http://www.meetmenow.webex.com

Yugma
https://www.yugma.com

INDEX

Made in the USA
Middletown, DE
06 October 2015